Bible Stories for Kids

Old Testament Adventures

Text written by Bradley Booth
Copyedited by Rudy Hall, Judy Jennings, Clarissa Fiedler
Edited by Lori Peckham, Jerry Stevens
Cover design by David Berthiaume
Interior design by Eric Pletcher
Cover illustrations by Leandro Tonelli, Javier Calvo
Additional design by Greg Solie • AltaGraph

Portions taken from the original works of E. G. White: *Patriarchs
and Prophets, Prophets and Kings, The Desire of Ages, The Acts
of the Apostles,* and *The Great Controversy.*

Printed in U.S.A.

ISBN: 978-1-5136-0135-9

Table of Contents

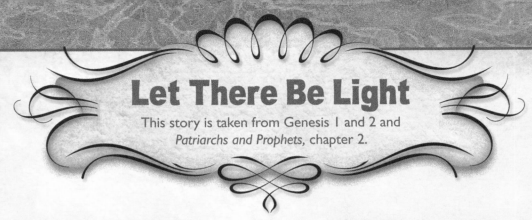

Let There Be Light

This story is taken from Genesis 1 and 2 and
Patriarchs and Prophets, chapter 2.

In the beginning God created the heavens and the earth" (Genesis 1:1). Wow! That's a tall order! How did He do that? How did He do it in six days, as the Bible says He did? We can read the whole incredible story in the book of Genesis.

In the beginning there was nothing. No people, no animals, no birds. There were no trees or flowers. No sun, moon, or stars. Not even any air or light. That is what the Bible says, and without anything in the world, it sounds like a pretty dark and scary place.

But the Father, Son, and Holy Spirit had a plan for this world. They were all there for the event. They all took part in choosing the exact spot in space for our new world.

The Son was the One who spoke everything into existence. He was and is equal to the Father and the Holy Spirit. He was the same Divine Person who would be born many centuries later in Bethlehem, the One we would call Jesus.

On the first day, God the Son made light. All was darkness until He spoke, and then suddenly the whole world was lit with the power of His glory. It pierced the blackness of that first morning and chased away every shadow in every corner of the world.

Twenty-four hours passed, and God enjoyed what He had made. Day and night made up that first day, and God said, "It is good." Now, when God says something is good, it must be very good.

The second day was much different from the first. By now, God's light was shining everywhere on our earth. The only thing that could be seen was water washing back and forth with the tides of the ocean and a mist covering the earth like a cloud of fog.

On the first day, God the Son made light. All was darkness until He spoke.

And God said, "Let there be a firmament between the waters to separate water from water." So God made the firmament and separated the water under the firmament from the water above it. God called the firmament "sky." How did that happen? Well, the mist surrounding the earth began to rise up and up and up until it formed the blue sky above. It was very scientific to be sure, but for God it was quite simple.

Now, on the third day things really began to happen, and if we had been there we would have been so surprised at all the changes that took place. God spoke, and the dry land rose up out of the waters, making hills, valleys, and plains. Everywhere on earth God formed streams. rivers, lakes, and small seas. They were not like the giant oceans we have today, but smaller ones that would help keep the earth's temperature just right all the time.

Not too hot during the day, and not too cold at night.

Then God spoke, and plants began to appear everywhere. He made flowers grow in the valleys and grass grow on the hills. He made trees fill the forests and algae form in the oceans.

He made daffodils, roses, petunias, and orchids. He made tall green grasses and short yellow grasses, and even some purple kinds. He made oak trees, maples, coconut palms, and towering pines. He made all the tiny microscopic plants in the ocean that whales would need for food, and green plankton to help the fish breathe.

He made plants that would grow food so that animals and people could eat, such as apple trees, tomato plants, and grape vines. All the things we love to taste grew on the plants God made that third day of Creation: corn and wheat, peaches and bananas, olives and nuts, pumpkins and watermelons. So many good things, and all from the Creator's hand.

> God spoke, and plants began to appear everywhere. He made flowers grow in the valleys and grass grow on the hills.

Best of all, He made these plants so they could grow seeds to make new plants just like themselves. Then we would never run out of all the good things every creature in this world would need for food.

Once again, 24 hours passed, and day turned into night. That was the end of the third day of Creation. God looked at everything He had made and decided that it was all very good—just the way He liked it. It was perfect in every way. He has all the power in the universe, so He is always perfect in everything He does. He made it that way because He loves us so much. We are very blessed indeed!

Creation week was such a special time for God! He had wanted to make our world for so long, and now it was actually happening. The first three days had been a wonderful time of celebration for God to show His love and awesome handiwork to the whole universe. By now, He had already made light, air, water, land, and plants, but He was only half

finished. Three more days of Creation week were yet to come.

As day four dawned, God did one of the most important things in all of Creation week. He made the lights that hang in the sky above our world. If we had been there that day, the first thing we would have seen was a ball of fire in the sky coming up over the horizon. It was our bright yellow sun, so nice and warm.

The sun would provide light for photosynthesis so that the green plants could grow. It would keep the earth's oceans and air temperatures warm everywhere in the world. It would also keep our bodies healthy so we wouldn't get sick.

Then as the sun went down in the western sky and it grew dark, another ball of orange came up over the horizon. It was our moon. As it rose in the night sky, it turned yellow and then finally white. There were other lights in the sky, too. Tiny pinpricks of light called stars could be seen all across the dark sky.

So God made the sun to rule the day and the moon to rule the night. God saw everything He had made on day four of Creation week and said, "It is good."

Day five dawned, and God must have been very excited. Until now, He had been making wonderful things, but none of them could sing, swim, or jump from branch to branch in a tree.

God said, "Let the waters be full of living creatures, and let birds fly above the earth

God did one of the most important things in all of Creation week. He made the lights that hang in the sky above our world.

across the sky." That is exactly what happened. Suddenly there were creatures everywhere in the waters of the earth—beautiful pink-colored salmon in the rivers, green trout in the lakes, and blue stingrays in the seas. Some water creatures swam together in schools like fish, and some just sat in beds on the bottom of the sea like oysters. Some floated with the water currents like jellyfish and sea horses. Others could jump right out of the water in big, arching half circles.

But God wasn't done. The sea creatures were only half of His creative works on day five. Soon creatures with wings and feathers appeared, and they came in all sizes. God made giant ostriches and tiny hummingbirds. He made some birds that chirped, some that quacked, and some that whistled. He made birds that built nests in the tops of trees, on the sides of cliffs, and in holes in the ground. Some birds were blue, some red, and some just plain brown. Some could hover and fly backward, and others could dive deep into the water. Some could even dive from thousands of feet in the sky.

The day turned to night, and some of the fish and birds that had been sleeping came out to eat and play. Twenty-four hours had passed by now, and God said, "It is good."

The sixth day dawned, and with it the final day of God's Creation. What a lot there was to do!

God thought of everything when He made all the creatures on day six. Some animals were very tall and others very short. Some animals could climb like monkeys. Others could jump like kangaroos. The porpoises could swim easily in the waters because they had airholes in the tops of their heads. The cheetahs and greyhounds could run like the wind. Hyenas could laugh, donkeys could bray, and whales could beep and moan. The flying squirrels could spread their feet and sail on the afternoon breezes.

God made all the creepy-crawly creatures on day six, too. He made the reptiles, the amphibians, the insects, and the cute little turtles.
He also made the elephants and whales as large as

God said, "Let the waters be full of living creatures."

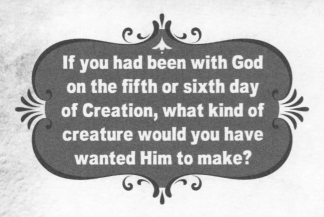

If you had been with God on the fifth or sixth day of Creation, what kind of creature would you have wanted Him to make?

a house. He designed the slippery, squishy salamanders and croaking, peeping frogs. He created buzzing bees, crawling beetles, and squirmy caterpillars that would turn into graceful butterflies.

God saw everything that He had made, and "It was good!" The day and evening had blended together to make another 24 hours, and all the creatures loved the new world God had made.

But He wasn't finished yet. The crowning act of His Creation was yet to come.

What a week it had turned out to be! The days of Creation had come and gone, bringing a whole new world to this part of our galaxy. Land, sea, and sky were now filled with plants, animals, and lights to give the earth a new look. And God said it was good.

However, He was saving the best for last as He put the finishing touches on His Creation week. God said, "Let Us make mankind in Our image, in Our likeness."

The Bible says He took dirt from the ground and shaped it in the form of a man. Then God did something He hadn't done for any other creature on earth. He breathed the very breath of heaven into the man. Now, that is really special!

Can you imagine that first day of life for Adam as he woke up and looked into the face of Jesus, his Maker? Can you see Jesus smiling at Adam and taking him by

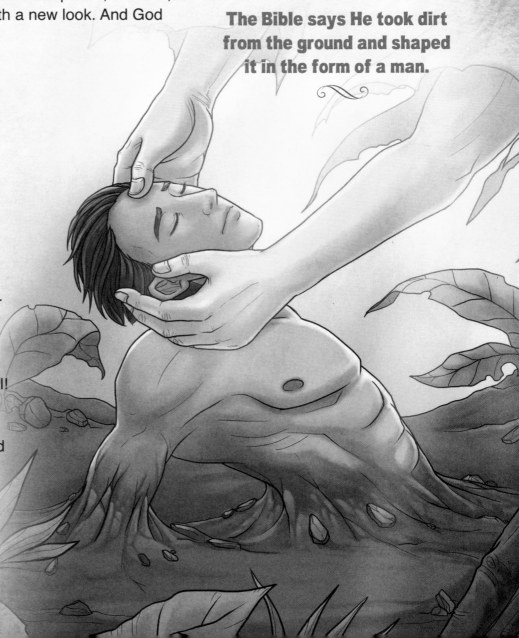

The Bible says He took dirt from the ground and shaped it in the form of a man.

the hand to lift him up? Can you see Adam, twice as tall as men today, strong, handsome, and dressed in a robe of light like the angels?

Jesus probably took him on a tour of the brand-new world, and what an experience that must have been! There was no one else to see it firsthand like Adam, because he was the only human being on earth.

Now Jesus brought the animals to Adam one by one to name them.

"What is this big animal with big furry hair all around its face?" Adam might have asked Him.

"That's a good question," Jesus likely replied. "I just made it, so it doesn't really have a name yet. What would you like to call an animal with such a big mouth and lots of teeth?"

And so it probably went throughout their walk that first day together. On every pathway in the woods was some new creature that astonished Adam. He marveled at the beautiful macaw parrot with its red, yellow, and blue feathers sitting on a perch in a woodland meadow. He was entertained by the game of tag the dolphins played in the bright blue lagoons. He was astonished at the shiny green serpent flying through the jungle.

When Adam woke up he was astonished at what he saw.

Adam named them all. God gave Adam the wisdom to name the animals according to how they looked, sounded, and walked. He named the birds, reptiles, and amphibians, too. He even named the fish and all the other creatures in the sea. How did he do all that in one day? I can't wait to get to heaven to ask him.

Then Adam began noticing something rather peculiar. In the various animal groups that swung from the trees, or raced across the plains, or played on the grass at his feet, there was always more than one of a kind in that

Like Adam and Eve, you have been made in the image of God. What does that mean to you?

They must have laughed together, and maybe even sung praises together.

group. There were herds of elephants. There were flocks of flamingos. There were schools of fish.

But there was only one human being, and Adam was it. Of course, God had a plan all along to take care of that.

He made Adam fall into a deep sleep. That must have been a very strange feeling for Adam because it was probably the first time he had gone to sleep.

While he slept, God did the very first surgery in history. He took one of Adam's ribs to make a woman, and when Adam woke up he was astonished at what he saw. She was the most elegant of God's creatures, the most beautiful, and the most lovely. She was God's crowning act of Creation. Dressed in a robe of light like Adam, she was the perfect match for him. And like Adam, she was made in the image of God.

What a wonderful way to end Creation week. Six days of Creation, and God saved the best part for last—a man and woman made in His image to rule the new world.

Creation week was finished, and God was done with all His work. The heavens and the earth had been created in just six short days—not millions or billions of years, as some scientists would have us believe. What a wonderful sign of God's creative power!

Can you imagine that first Friday evening in the new garden home? God called it Eden, and He gave it to our first parents as a wedding present. Beautiful streams cascaded through sunlit woods strewn with flowers of every color. Tall hills with even taller trees pointed to a sky filled with fleecy white clouds. Deep blue seas and lakes across God's green earth were decorated with plenty of animals, birds, and fish to make the world picture-perfect.

Adam and Eve were married on that first day in Eden, and God performed the very first wedding ceremony! What a special memory that must have been for them! They must have walked for hours climbing grassy hills and

wading through cool, flowing streams. Maybe they stopped to play with tigers, listened to whip-poor-wills sing, or climbed a tree to eat a peach. Whatever they did, the experience must have been exciting! The gifts of sight, sound, taste, smell, and touch were all given to the first couple to make their lives wonderfully complete.

But the best part was yet to come. As the sun began to set that first Friday evening, God the Son called Adam and Eve to come sit with Him. They may have gone to talk on a high hill overlooking deep valleys to the west, or it may have been on the sandy shore of some beautiful lake reflecting the colors of sunset.

Adam and Eve must have bowed their heads in reverence for their Creator.

They must have talked about all the wonderful things they had seen that first day. They must have laughed together, and maybe even sung praises together in celebration of all that God had given them. And that would have been their first sunset vespers together with their marvelous Creator! When the sun dipped below the horizon with its glorious pinks, oranges, and reds, Adam and Eve must have held their breath at all that splendor! And to think that God had made it for them!

That Friday sunset marked the beginning of something God called the Sabbath day. It was a time for Adam and Eve to set aside all their work and daily activities to be with their Creator.

The Bible tells us exactly how it happened. By the seventh day, God had finished the work He had been doing, and He rested from all His work. Then God blessed the seventh day and made it holy.

That night Adam and Eve went to sleep for the first time in their very own garden. They probably slept on the nice soft grass with sweet-smelling flowers and the pale yellow

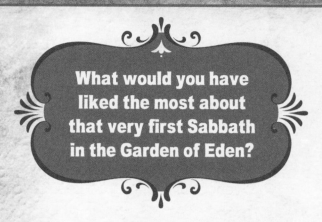

What would you have liked the most about that very first Sabbath in the Garden of Eden?

moon bathing their garden home in its soft light.

The next day dawned with a mist that rose into the warm morning air. By the time Adam and Eve had eaten their breakfast of mangoes and strawberries, the mist would have cleared to show purple-headed hills under a deep blue sky. God the Son spent the day with them, and I'm sure they invited the angels to come along too as they walked the forest trails.

When they stopped to pick the roses and smell them one by one, I can imagine God smiling. It must have made Him happy to see them enjoying the world so much. When they sat by a stream and let the fish nibble on their toes, they must have all laughed. When they heard the robins sing their morning songs, they must have bowed their heads in reverence for their Creator who could make things so wonderfully perfect!

Today, we remember that first Sabbath when God rested in celebration of all He had created. Like Adam and Eve, we worship Him in honor of that day. It is a day to remember all of the wonderful things that He made for us. It is a day to remember that He loves us. Aren't you glad He made the Sabbath?

Talking with Jesus:

"Dear Jesus, I am so glad You made this wonderful world and that I get to be a part of it, help me treat the Sabbath as the holy day You intended it to be."

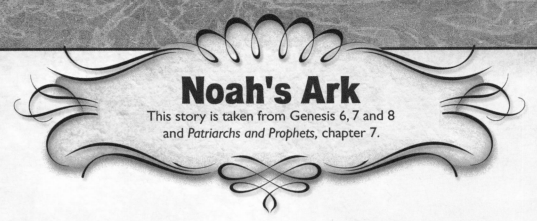

Noah's Ark

This story is taken from Genesis 6, 7 and 8
and *Patriarchs and Prophets,* chapter 7.

Long ago, our earth was a much nicer place to live. The wonderful climate was never too hot and never too cold. There was always plenty to eat. People never got sick; in fact, they should have lived forever. It was what God had always wanted for His creatures on earth, but because of sin, everything was no longer perfect.

Adam and Eve had believed Satan's lies. They had doubted God and eaten the forbidden fruit in the garden, which brought sadness and separation from their Creator. The results of sin were now apparent everywhere. Leaves fell from the trees, and the flowers faded. Animals hunted each other for food. People became more and more evil and fought among themselves.

Everything and everyone got old. People would now die, and so would animals and plants. Without the fruit from the tree of life in the Garden of Eden, people could not live forever, as God had originally intended.

Everyone should have been drawing closer to God and feeling sad for all the troubles that were coming on the earth because of sin. Instead, they rebelled against God even more. God saw how great the wickedness of the human race had become and that every thought of their hearts was evil all the time.

People were doing so many bad things and sometimes acted more like animals than humans. They partied and drank alcohol until it made them do all kinds of horrible things. If they wanted something, they took it by force. Sometimes it was money. Sometimes it was land. Sometimes they kidnapped women or children. There was great violence on earth, and people often killed each other just for sport. Wars were being fought everywhere between clans, tribes, and nations. Bad people began to hunt the good people down to exterminate them. There were many other evil things that we cannot even imagine.

God told Noah, "Make yourself an ark of gopherwood. Make rooms in the ark, and cover it inside and outside with pitch."

To eliminate all of this wickedness, God decided that He would have to send a flood of waters on the earth to destroy all the evil people. That was a very hard thing for Him to do because He had created the world, and He loved it. But there was nothing else He could do. If He allowed the wickedness to go unpunished, soon there wouldn't be any people left on the earth at all.

So God called on a man named Noah. He was one of the few righteous people left on the earth. The Bible says, "Noah walked with God." God knew He could completely trust Noah to do whatever He asked.

God told Noah, "Make yourself an ark, or boat, of gopherwood. Make rooms in the ark, and cover it inside and outside with pitch. The length of the ark shall be 300 cubits, its width 50 cubits, and its height 30 cubits." A cubit is approximately 18 inches, so that means the ark was approximately 450 feet long, 75 feet wide, and 45 feet high. Wow! That is a really big boat!

Why such a huge boat? Because God wanted anyone who believed in Him and wanted to be saved from the flood to have a chance to get on board the ark and be safe. Also, God loved animals, and the boat had to be big enough for His plan to save the animals and their food, too.

What must it have been like to see all those animals coming on the ark?

The gopherwood Noah used to build the ark was very hard. Ordinary saws that we use today would have had a hard time cutting it.

For 120 years, Noah and his sons were building the ark, and while they worked, Noah preached warning messages of the disaster to come. Crowds gathered around the ark as though it was some kind of a carnival, and Noah no doubt stood on a pile of lumber or some other high place so that everyone could see and hear him. He wanted everyone to hear his message of warning and believe.

Most people didn't care much about what Noah had to say. They just laughed and called him a foolish old man. Many famous scientists probably came to listen to Noah and to argue with him, too. In those days, there was more land than water. They asked, "How could a flood of waters destroy the world when there isn't enough water on earth to do it? Why would God destroy the beautiful world that He created only a few centuries ago, anyway?"

Besides all that, people were so busy building houses, running businesses, getting married, and going on vacation that they scarcely had time to worry much about Noah's warnings about a flood. And, of course, some just wanted to make trouble for Noah. But God protected him and kept him from harm and danger.

When the ark was finally finished, Noah must have breathed a sigh of relief. Now he needed to get all the animals and birds on board, but how was he going to do that?

Imagine his surprise one day to see the animals coming from every direction toward the ark, walking in perfect order. Some came by twos and some by sevens. Birds swarmed to the ark, darkening the skies as they came, drawn by some mysterious power.

The people standing around were shocked and awed by such a sight. It was clear that a supernatural power was attending the animals, guiding them to the ark so that Noah and his sons could shut them up in their pens and cages.

When the last animal was on the ark, Noah came out and gave one last invitation from the doorway of the ark. "Please come into the ark while you have the opportunity!" he pleaded. "Now is the day of salvation!"

Would anyone accept his message of hope and safety? Noah wondered. Would they come on board to escape the approaching flood?

Imagine Noah's surprise to see the animals coming from every direction toward the ark, walking in perfect order.

Noah stood in the doorway of the ark, waiting for people to join him on board. "Will no one accept God's invitation of mercy and find safety in the ark?" he shouted. "A terrible flood is on its way! Please join us on board now before it's too late!"

Sadly, no one took him up on the offer. Only his wife, his three sons, and his sons' wives walked up that ramp and into the ark. He couldn't believe it. He had been warning and pleading with these people for 120 years. Now was coming a flood so terrible that it would swallow an entire world. All the people had to do to be safe was to take a short walk up the ramp and get into the ark, but no one would listen. They would all be lost, and there was nothing more Noah could do but to get into the ark as God had told him.

As Noah disappeared inside the ark, a hush settled over the crowd.

Then suddenly a bright flash of light streaked down from the sky and rested motionless by the open doorway of the ark. The crowds stood dumbstruck at the glorious being, but still no one made a move forward to enter the door of the ark.

Slowly the giant door began to swing shut on its hinges. An unseen hand was closing it until it hit the side of the ark with a thud.

"There will be no flood," they told one another, and soon they were smiling and laughing as before.

"Open the door!" they screamed.
"We're sorry we didn't listen!
Open the door, or we'll drown!"

For seven days, the people shouted and made fun of Noah. I can almost hear them saying, "You've lost your mind. What a fool to be sitting in that ark with all of those smelly animals."

However, one week later their day of judgment came. Suddenly a stiff wind began to blow, and dark clouds rolled up on the horizon. The people had never seen such things before. When lightning raced across the sky and big raindrops began to fall, they grew really worried. The earth itself seemed to break apart as geysers of water came shooting from the ground. Heavy rain and hail fell from the sky, and huge tsunami waves rushed over the land.

Some people rushed to the ark to call on Noah. "Open the door!" they screamed. "We're sorry we didn't listen! Open the door, or we'll drown!" But Noah could not open the heavy door that God's power had closed. It was too late.

People and animals were running everywhere now trying to find a safe place. Some climbed up on their houses, and some climbed trees. Others ran to the highest hills to get away from the rising water. People and animals fought together to escape the flood, but one by one they lost their foothold and fell away into the swirling waters.

Some tried to hang on to the ark and some tried to climb up on it, but the rising tide of waters quickly tore the desperate victims from its side. Soon there was nothing left but the howling winds and the ark plunging up and down on the churning waters. Not a man, woman, or child could be seen anywhere. Not a horse or a lion. There was no living thing in sight.

Meanwhile, Noah and his family were doing all they could to calm down the animals inside. No one had ever experienced anything like this before, so they didn't know what to expect. Noah prayed. It was all anyone could do. Satan and his evil angels tried to sink the ark, but

Noah opened a window in the ark and sent out a raven and then a dove to see what would happen.

God and His holy angels protected the small crew and their boatload of animals.

For 40 days and nights, the rains fell from the sky, and the waters rose still higher. Finally, the tops of the highest mountains on earth were more than 20 feet beneath the waves. The terrible flood that Noah had preached about had come, and just as he had warned, no living thing outside the ark remained alive.

For months, the ark drifted back and forth on the endless ocean. There was lots of food stored on the ark, so there was plenty to eat, but there was also plenty of work. Noah and his family had to feed all those animals! Every day! They had to clean their stalls and cages too. What a smelly job!

They all watched for signs that the flood might be nearing its end. After a time, God sent winds to start drying up the water. Finally, the ark stopped moving and came to rest on the Mountains of Ararat. What a relief. It had been 10 months now. The tops of the mountains could be seen, and the sun was shining.

Noah opened a window in the ark and sent out a raven and then a dove to see what would happen. The raven never came back, but the dove returned. A week later Noah sent out the dove again, and it soon returned with an olive leaf in its beak. Plants were growing again. The third time Noah sent out the dove it did not return, and Noah knew there must be lots of dry land all over the earth.

Before starting to build himself a home, Noah led out in a worship of praise to God.

Finally, more than a year after Noah and his family had entered the ark, the giant door slowly began to open. An angel of God had come to let them out. They were so happy! God had been watching over them, and He would let them out of the ark only when earth's conditions were right for survival.

The animals ran from their cages, happy to be free at last. A few stayed around the ark, content to remain with the people who had cared for them for so long.

Why did God give us the rainbow?

Before starting to build himself a home, Noah led out in a worship of praise to God. He offered sacrifices, they probably sang some songs, and the Lord drew very near to them. "I will never again destroy the earth with floodwaters," God told Noah's family, "and that's a promise."

They bowed their heads in prayer to thank God for His care and protection during the long months of the flood. As their prayer ended, they all looked up and saw an amazing sight. Stretched above them over the ark was a beautiful rainbow in the clouds. The first one ever!

And this wasn't just any rainbow! It was much more than that! It was a promise from God that the whole world would never again be destroyed by a flood. So every time we see a rainbow, it is a reminder of our loving Savior, who always keeps His promises.

Talking with Jesus:

"Thank You, Lord, for sending us the rainbow as a reminder of Your promise. We know we can trust You to keep Your word. Help us to always listen to You."

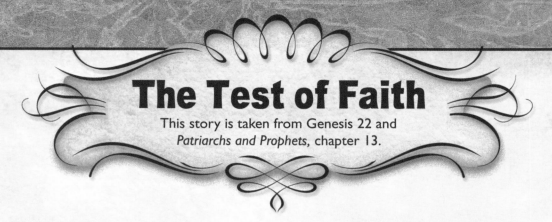

The Test of Faith

This story is taken from Genesis 22 and
Patriarchs and Prophets, chapter 13.

God blessed Abraham, and the boy He had been promising him for 25 years was finally born. Abraham thought having a son was no longer possible for him because he was 100 years old. But God had promised that he would have a son by Sarah, and that is exactly what happened.

They called him Isaac, and what joy he brought to Abraham and Sarah in their old age. Can you imagine Isaac helping Abraham with the sheep at shearing time? Can you see him sitting with Sarah around the evening campfires? Everybody grew so attached to the boy; they probably wondered how they had ever lived without him.

Isaac was such a cheerful boy. He was obedient and willing to help do chores around the camp when asked. When it came to spiritual things, he was like his father, Abraham—always ready to learn and always willing to accept God's leading in his life.

Then one night while Abraham was on one of his long walks under the starry skies, God made a very hard request of him. "Take Isaac, your only son whom you dearly love, and go to the hills of Moriah. There I want you to sacrifice him as a burnt offering on a mountain that I will show you."

Can you imagine what must have been going through Abraham's mind when he heard God's command? Was God really asking him to offer his son like a lamb as a sacrifice on an altar? Pagan nations around him did this sometimes, but worshippers of Jehovah had never been asked to do such a thing! It seemed an impossible request of God, and Abraham must have struggled with this in prayer. Again and again he must have asked God why, but there was no further word from heaven.

So the next morning before daybreak, Abraham got up and woke Isaac. They cut the wood that they would need for the burnt offering and loaded it on a donkey, along with a tent and enough food for the three-day trip. Then, taking two servants with them, the father and son left for the hills of Moriah.

Abraham told no one why they were making this journey. For one thing, he didn't know how to break the bad news. For another, he probably thought it was just a bad dream, or maybe God would somehow change His mind.

The two of them had probably taken many trips together, but never one like this. Unless God intervened, Abraham knew this would be their last trip

Abraham thought having a son with Sarah was no longer possible for him because he was 100 years old. But that is exactly what happened.

together, and it must have broken his heart.

On the third day the hills of Moriah could be seen in the distance, and Abraham told the servants to stop and take a break. "Stay here with the donkey while Isaac and I go up on the mountain. We will worship the Lord and offer our sacrifice, and then we will return to you," he said.

Isaac started up the mountain with the bundle of wood, and Abraham went along behind him with a knife and the coals that they would need to start a fire.

Can you imagine how hard that climb must have been for Abraham, who loved his son so much? "Please, Lord, spare me my son!" he must have prayed as they walked up that mountain. Again, God did not answer. This was a test to see if Abraham would obey God, even though he felt as if God was asking for something impossible.

At some point along the trail when they stopped to rest, Isaac looked at his father. "We have the wood for the sacrifice and the fire," he said, "but where is the lamb for the burnt offering?"

They loaded the wood on the donkey, along with a tent and enough food for the three-day trip.

Abraham didn't know what to say. Soon he would have to break the terrible news, but he just couldn't bring himself to say it yet. For now Abraham could say only, "God will provide the lamb for our burnt offering, my son." Then the two of them went on together.

When they reached the place God had chosen for the sacrifice, Abraham and Isaac built an altar from stones and put the wood on it. Then with tears in his eyes, Abraham explained what God had asked him to do.

Isaac was afraid at first, but like his father he had a good relationship with God. "If that is what God told you to do, then we must obey Him," Isaac finally said.

Can't you see the two of them standing there on the mountain talking about God's command to offer Isaac as a sacrifice? What they didn't know was that God had asked Abraham to sacrifice his son as a lesson for all the unfallen worlds of the universe to see.

Someday our heavenly Father would send His only Son Jesus to give His life as a sacrifice for the world. And this test of faith for Abraham made that promise very real.

Abraham's hands were shaking by now, but Isaac helped his father be strong. He was young and could have run away, but he had been raised to trust God, even if he didn't fully understand His command.

Suddenly, he heard a voice from heaven. "Abraham! Abraham! Don't harm the boy. Now I know that you love Me."

Isaac climbed up on the wood of the altar, ready to die as God had asked him to do. What a picture they must have made, as father and son hugged each other goodbye.

"Lord, this is such a hard thing to do!" Abraham must have prayed one last time as he looked to heaven. "I do not want to do this, but I will do it because You have asked. I know You can even raise Isaac from the dead if You want." You can be sure by now that Abraham had tears streaming down his face as he took the knife and raised it above his son.

Then the miracle happened, just as Abraham had hoped it would. Suddenly, he heard a voice from heaven. "Abraham! Abraham! Don't harm the boy. Now I know that you love Me because you have not withheld from Me your

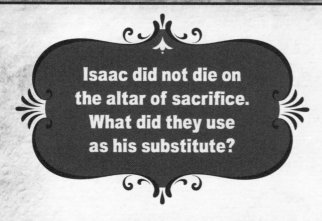

Isaac did not die on the altar of sacrifice. What did they use as his substitute?

only son. You have proven yourself to be a man of faith because you have obeyed My voice."

God had answered Abraham's prayer. At that very moment, Abraham heard the bleating of a ram nearby caught by its horns in a thorny thicket. So he took the ram and sacrificed it as a burnt offering instead of his son.

As with Abraham, God often asks us to do things that we don't understand. He gives us instructions in the Bible and then expects us to obey them. Why? Because He knows best. He can see what lies ahead, and He wants us to grow in grace. He wants our faith in Him to grow stronger and our characters to become more like His. If we obey Him, even when what He is asking doesn't seem to make sense, we will grow close to God like Abraham did.

Talking with Jesus:

"Dear Father in heaven, thank You for this amazing story that shows us how much You love us."

Joseph's Coat and Dreams

This story is taken from Genesis 37, 39-45 and *Patriarchs and Prophets*, chapter 19-21.

O f all Jacob's sons, Joseph was his favorite. His being Jacob's favorite did not make him very popular with his 10 older brothers.

Jacob's own childhood experiences should have taught him that having a favorite child wasn't wise. He had always been his mother's favorite, while Esau had been Isaac's favorite. We know what kind of trouble that made for Jacob and Esau.

However, try as he might, Jacob could not help but show how much he loved and preferred Joseph to the others. Joseph and his younger brother, Benjamin, were from Jacob's favorite wife, Rachel.

Then Jacob made the biggest mistake of all. He wove a fine robe for Joseph that was truly worthy of a royal prince. This, of course, made the 10 older brothers even more jealous.

To make matters worse, one day Joseph told his brothers about a dream he had had. "We were in a field binding sheaves of grain," he said, "and suddenly my sheaf stood up straight and your sheaves all bowed down to mine."

Now his brothers were angry. "Do you think you are going to rule over us?" they scoffed.

Then Joseph had another dream, and he told his brothers about that one, too. "In my second dream the sun, moon, and 11 stars all bowed down to me," he said.

The brothers were even angrier about this dream, and even Jacob scolded Joseph when he heard about the dreams.

Of course, no one really knew what the dreams meant at that time, or if they meant anything at all, but someday they would all remember the dreams very clearly.

Jacob wove a fine robe for Joseph that was truly worthy of a royal prince.

Meanwhile, there was lots to do in a tent village like the one Joseph lived in. Donkeys and oxen needed to plow the soil for crops of wheat and barley. Camels needed to be loaded for journeys in merchant caravans. Sheep needed to be sheared, watered, and grazed.

One day Joseph was asked to go check on his older brothers, who had taken the flocks and herds to be grazed far from home. "Take your brothers some food and check on them to see how they are doing," Jacob said. Little did he know that this would be the last time he would see Joseph for 22 years.

Joseph walked to a town called Shechem but couldn't find his brothers there. "I heard

them say they were going to Dothan," a man told Joseph when he found the boy wandering in a field.

So Joseph traveled on to Dothan. He was so excited to find his brothers when he recognized them in the distance, but they were not excited to see him. "Here comes that dreamer!" they muttered. "Let's kill him and throw him into one of the deep pits around here! We can say a wild animal ate him! Then we will see what becomes of his dreams!"

Reuben was frightened by such a thought. "Let's not kill him," he said. "Let's just throw him into a pit and leave him there to die!" Secretly, Reuben was planning to let him out later and send him back home to his father.

The brothers were even angrier about this dream, and even Jacob scolded Joseph.

When Joseph finally arrived in camp, the brothers grabbed him, stripped off his beautiful coat, and threw him into a pit.

The pit was empty, with no water in it. It was deep and scary. Can you imagine how frightened Joseph must have been?

What were his brothers doing? he wondered. Why were they treating him this way? How long would it be before they let him out?

"Please let me out!" he must have begged again and again.

As the hours passed and the brothers sat down to eat the food he had brought them, Joseph began to get even more scared. What if his brothers never let him out? What if they headed off with the cattle and sheep and forgot all about him? How long could he last in this pit with no water or food?

Then the plot changed because the brothers spotted a caravan of Ishmaelite traders coming down the road. "Hey, I've got

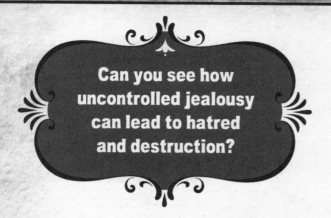

an idea!" Judah announced. "Why don't we sell Joseph as a slave? If we kill him, we will get nothing, but if we sell him to the traders, we can make a little money off of him. After all, he is our brother, our own flesh and blood."

So they dragged Joseph up out of the hole. He was dirty and tired, but relieved that they were finally letting him out. However, when he realized what they were doing, his cries became frantic again. "Please don't sell me as a slave!" he must have pleaded. "Being a slave is worse than death!"

But they sold him anyway for 20 pieces of silver. What a sad, pitiful price that was! Two pieces of silver for each of the brothers. That little bit of money couldn't have lasted them more than a few weeks at most.

Reuben happened to be away when Joseph was sold. Maybe he was watering the sheep, or maybe he was giving instructions to the other herdsmen. However, when he discovered what the other brothers had done, he was astonished and tore his clothes! "How could you do this!" we can imagine him shouting at his brothers. "While we still had Joseph there was a way out of this mess! Now we have got nothing but a few pieces of silver to show for our terrible deed!"

But what was done was done. So after some discussion the brothers killed a goat and dipped Joseph's coat in it. Then they took it back home to Jacob and showed it to him.

"We found this along the road," they said, "and were wondering if it might be Joseph's."

The brothers hadn't really thought much about how badly this news would affect their father, but the reaction they got when they told him was a nightmare!

"Oh, no!" Jacob began to wail as though he were already at Joseph's funeral. "It is my son's robe! Surely some ferocious animal has attacked and killed him! Joseph has been

They dragged Joseph up out of the hole. He was dirty and tired, but relieved that they were finally letting him out.

torn to pieces!"

They tried to comfort Jacob, but he just waved them all off. He tore his clothes, as was the custom in those days, put on sackcloth, and sobbed and sobbed as though his heart would break. For months he mourned the loss of Joseph, and there was nothing anyone could do to relieve his suffering.

"In mourning will I go down to the grave!" he cried.

Can you imagine selling your own brother as a slave because of all the hate and jealousy you have in your heart? Nevertheless, his brothers made that decision, and they had to live with it for the rest of their lives.

Joseph was on his way to Egypt, leaving behind everything that was familiar. How could his brothers have sold him as a slave? It all seemed like a dream now. He had traveled so far to bring them food! He had been so excited to see them, and so surprised to see their looks of anger when he finally arrived.

The camel caravan was passing west of Hebron now, and Joseph could see the hills in the distance where his father's tents were pitched. He was so close and

One day Potiphar's wife approached Joseph and tempted him to be unfaithful to God.

yet so far away. Would he ever see his father again?

With terror and overwhelming grief, he turned his eyes to Egypt. What would become of him in that strange land? How would he be treated? He would be all alone, and that thought made him want to panic!

He remembered all that his father had taught him about God and the heavenly angels who care for His people wherever they go. So he vowed that he would be faithful to the God of Abraham, Isaac, and Jacob, even if he was going to be a slave.

In Egypt, the Ishmaelite slave traders sold Joseph to Potiphar, the captain of Pharaoh's guard. That was a good thing for Joseph because there was less of a chance that he would have to work in the fields now. He was able to read too, and this made it possible for him to use such skills to help run the household.

Sure enough, it wasn't long before he was doing many things to make Potiphar prosper. Joseph was an honest man, and Potiphar could see that. Everything went so well that soon he put Joseph in charge of managing his entire household.

However, trouble was on the way. One day Potiphar's wife approached Joseph and tempted him to be unfaithful to God. The temptation was strong, and Joseph knew that if he did as she wished, he would be rewarded. If he refused, he would probably be sent to prison and maybe even executed.

Joseph knew he could not disobey God. He would rather have God's favor than all the fame and riches in the world.

When Potiphar's wife realized that Joseph could not be tempted to do wrong, she called in the servants and told them that Joseph had attacked her. Immediately, he was sent to prison for a crime he did not commit.

We can imagine that he was tempted to think the Lord had abandoned him, but he knew that God wasn't like that. Hard as it was, Joseph determined once again that he would always stand for the right, no matter the consequences.

While in prison Joseph helped the warden, and God blessed him. Soon he was in charge of the prisoners.

One morning he noticed that two of the prisoners were looking sad, so he asked if he

"We had dreams last night, and they were very troubling," said the two prisoners.

How would you have felt if you had been sold as a slave to the Egyptians?

could be of any help. Both of the prisoners had worked for Pharaoh in his royal palace—the royal cupbearer and the chief baker—but they had been accused of crimes and thrown into prison.

"We had dreams last night, and they were very troubling," said the two prisoners, "but there is no one to interpret them for us."

"God can interpret your dreams," Joseph said confidently. "Tell me what you saw." The cupbearer shared his dream first. "I dreamed I saw three bunches of grapes on a vine, and I squeezed the juice from the grapes into Pharaoh's cup."

Joseph smiled at the cupbearer. "The three bunches of grapes are three days. In three days Pharaoh will give you back your old job in the palace," he said. "Please, when you have settled into your old job again, remember me here in this prison and speak a good word for me to Pharaoh."

"Can we find anyone like Joseph, in whom is found the spirit of God?" said Pharaoh.

The baker then told Joseph his dream. "On my head were three baskets of bread, and the birds were eating the baked things out of the top basket," he said.

Joseph's face grew serious as he heard the dream, but the baker insisted he interpret it as he had for the cupbearer. "The three baskets you saw are also three days," Joseph said, "but I am sad to tell you that in three days Pharaoh is going to have you executed."

Amazingly, the interpretations proved to be accurate. Pharaoh's birthday celebration came three days later. On that day he returned the cupbearer to his position in the court but executed the baker.

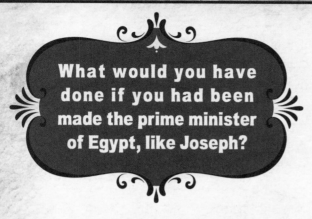

What would you have done if you had been made the prime minister of Egypt, like Joseph?

Unfortunately, the cupbearer promptly forgot all about the one who had helped him, so Joseph ended up spending another two years in prison.

However, one morning he awoke with a start when a guard rushed into the prison. "Get yourself cleaned up!" he ordered. "Pharaoh has ordered you to appear before him at once!"

Evidently, the cupbearer had remembered his promise to Joseph and told Pharaoh about the Hebrew slave who could interpret dreams. Within minutes, Joseph was rushed off to the palace to hear the dreams for himself.

"In my first dream, I saw seven fat cows come out of the river," said Pharaoh. "After them came seven skinny cows, and then the strangest thing happened. The seven skinny cows ate up all the fat cows. Even after they ate the fat cows up, they looked just as skinny as before."

He continued, "In my second dream, I saw seven heads of grain coming up ripe and ready to harvest. After them, seven other heads of grain sprouted, but they were all withered and thin from the hot desert winds. The thin heads of grain swallowed up the seven good heads. The dreams are very troubling," Pharaoh said, "but there is no one among all my wise men who can interpret them for me."

"Your dreams both mean the same thing," said Joseph. "God is telling you what He is about to do. The seven fat cows and full heads of grain are seven years of plenty. The seven lean cows and withered grain are seven years of famine. It means seven years of good crops will come, and then seven years of famine will follow. The years of famine will be so bad that everyone will forget the years of plenty.

"The Pharaoh should now choose a wise man and put him in charge of all the land of Egypt," said Joseph. "Let him appoint officers to take one-fifth of all the harvests for the next seven years and store them in big warehouses. This grain will then be used for food during the coming famine. That way the land of Egypt will not be ruined by the coming disaster."

Whom did Pharaoh choose to do this job for him? None other than Joseph. "Can we find anyone like this man, in whom is found the Spirit of God?" said Pharaoh.

So Joseph, once a prince of Canaan and then a slave, became the prime minister of Egypt. And all because he trusted in the Lord God of Abraham, Isaac, and Jacob.

The years of plenty came and went, just as Joseph had predicted. As planned, everyone brought one-fifth of their crop to Joseph so it could be stored in giant granaries all over Egypt. Fortunately, by the end of the good years, the granaries were full to overflowing.

Then came the years of poor crops or no harvests at all. The famine in Egypt was turning out to be really bad, but it was also being felt in many surrounding countries. Before long, everyone's food supplies had been used up.

Meanwhile, in Canaan Jacob and his sons were asking themselves what they should do. "I have heard that there is grain in Egypt," Jacob said to his sons. "Go down there and buy some for us, so that we may live and not die."

So Jacob's 10 oldest sons saddled their donkeys and went to Egypt to buy grain. When they got there, they were told to see the governor, who was the overseer of all grain supplies. They didn't know it, but the governor was their brother Joseph. When they came into his presence, they bowed to the ground to show respect, as was customary in those days.

Joseph remembered his dreams from so long ago about his brothers bowing to him.

Joseph recognized his brothers, and he also remembered his dreams from so long ago about his brothers bowing to him. Obviously they did not recognize him. Were they the same men they had been years before when they sold him into slavery? Were they still cruel and hateful, or were they kind and unselfish now?

Joseph decided he would give his brothers a test. "I think you are spies," he told them through an interpreter.

"No, my lord, we have come to buy food," they said. "We are honest men."

"I think that you have come to spy on Egypt," Joseph insisted. "Where do you come from, and how many are there in your family?"

"We were 12 brothers from one family in Canaan."

"Is your father still living?" Joseph was persistent.

"Our father is living, and our youngest brother is with

Why did Joseph ask his brothers to bring Benjamin to Egypt?

him, but one other brother is no longer alive."

"You are spies, and I think you are lying. Therefore, I will put you to the test. One of you may go home to bring the youngest son while the rest of you are kept here in prison."

After three days, Joseph finally let them out of prison. He dared not keep them any longer because he knew the family in Canaan might starve without food.

"This is how you will prove you are honest men," he told his brothers. "The next time you come back to Egypt, bring your youngest brother. In the meantime, one of you will stay here as a guarantee that the others will return. You will stay behind in prison!" he said, pointing at Simeon.

To the brothers, it seemed as if things were going from bad to worse. They had come to Egypt just to get grain, but now they had been accused of being spies. And they all knew that Simeon had been the brother who had come up with the idea of selling Joseph as a slave.

"God is punishing us because we sold Joseph into slavery!" said Reuben. "I begged you to spare him, but you wouldn't listen. Now that terrible deed has come back to haunt us tenfold!"

"One of you has stolen the governor's silver cup!"

And so the nine brothers left Egypt, but that night to their horror they found the silver they had paid for the grain in the tops of their sacks. They didn't know it, but Joseph had ordered his servants to put the silver there.

Horrified, the brothers continued on their way home, vowing they would pay double for their grain the next time they returned to Egypt.

When they finally reached home in Canaan, they told Jacob all about their trip. They told him that the governor had imprisoned them for three days because he thought they were spies. They told him about the silver in their grain sacks, and why Simeon was not with them, and that they could not go back to Egypt again without Benjamin.

Of course, Jacob was stunned that Simeon was locked up in prison, but he was even more afraid of letting Benjamin go to Egypt.

"My youngest son will not go down there with you! His older brother is dead, and now you want to take Benjamin, too! Absolutely not! If something should happen to him, it would kill me for sure."

Time passed, and the supplies of food ran low again. Jacob kept saying he wouldn't let Benjamin travel with the brothers, but in the end, he had no choice. If he didn't let him go, they would all starve.

Sending everyone but his brothers out of the room, he told them, "I am Joseph."

So they made the trip to Egypt once again, and when Joseph saw Benjamin, he ordered them to come to his house as guests.

The brothers came to his home trembling, fearful of what might come next. They apologized to the governor's steward for the silver they had found in their sacks, but he waved off their explanations, telling them the silver was a blessing from their God.

When they gave Joseph gifts of honey, spices, and pistachio nuts from their father, the governor asked about Jacob, and they told him that their father was doing well.

Simeon was brought out to them now, and the brothers were so happy to see him after so many weeks. Joseph could hardly hold back the tears when he saw his younger brother, Benjamin, and he had to leave the room.

The brothers were then placed at the table in the order of their age, and this astonished them. The fact

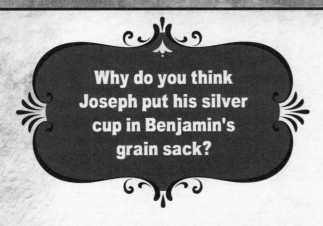

Why do you think Joseph put his silver cup in Benjamin's grain sack?

that the governor knew so many details about their family frightened them.

The next day at dawn, the brothers were finally sent on their way. However, they hadn't gotten far down the road when the governor's steward came after them.

"One of you has stolen the governor's silver cup!" he shouted.

Everyone protested that such a thing was impossible, but when the cup was found in Benjamin's sack, they all went back to Joseph's home, sick at heart about what was coming.

"You have returned my kindness with wickedness!" he scolded them. "For this, the guilty one must remain behind in prison."

"We are good men," Judah protested, "but how can we prove our innocence? We don't know how all these things have happened as you say they did. Please, do not take our youngest brother as a slave. If you do this, it will kill our father, who is already old. Let me stay in the young man's place. I will bear the blame for the cup being in his sack."

Joseph could hide his identity no longer. He had wanted to know if his brothers had changed, and now he knew. Sending everyone but his brothers out of the room, he told them, "I am Joseph."

The brothers were terrified, but he assured them that the evil they had intended for him had been turned to good. God had blessed Joseph. Now he was the prime minister of Egypt and could help save thousands of lives from starvation.

Talking with Jesus:

"Dear God of Abraham, Isaac, and Jacob, help me to be faithful to You always, no matter what life brings my way."

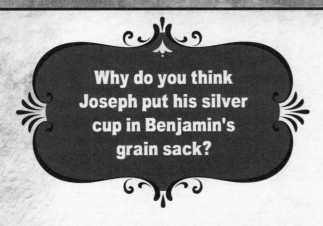

Victory Over the Midianites

This story is taken from Judges 7 and 8 and
Patriarchs and Prophets, chapter 53.

Gideon and his 300 men were ready for battle now. He had heard the message that God wanted him to hear in the Midianite soldier's dream. There was no doubt in his mind that God would help him win the battle. He was so overwhelmed with God's promise of a coming victory that he bowed his face to the ground to thank Him.

Then he went back to his camp of sleeping soldiers and woke them up. "Get up!" he said. "The Lord has delivered the camp of Midian into your hand."

He divided his soldiers into three groups. Into each man's hand he put a trumpet and an empty clay jar with a torch inside.

"Follow my lead!" he ordered his men. "When I and my group of 100 get to the edge of the Midianite camp, we will blow our trumpets and break our clay jars to reveal our lighted torches. That will be the signal for every group on every side to blow their trumpets, break their clay jars, and shout, 'The sword of the Lord and of Gideon!'"

Gideon divided his soldiers into three groups. Into each man's hand he put a trumpet and an empty clay jar with a torch inside.

Gideon and his 100 soldiers reached the edge of the camp at the beginning of the middle watch, just after the changing of the guard. Everyone in the camp was sound asleep except the few guards keeping watch. Not a sound could be heard except the night crickets and the crackling of the campfires.

Suddenly Gideon blew his trumpet, and all three companies blew their trumpets and then smashed their jars. Grasping the torches in their left hands and holding the trumpets in their right hands, they shouted, "The sword of the Lord and of Gideon!"

By now Gideon and his men had surrounded the Midianite camp. The Midianites woke up from their sleep and didn't know what to do. They must have thought they were being overrun by tens of thousands of enemy Israelites, because all they could see was a ring of torches encircling the camp.

In a panic, they began running in every direction. But Gideon and his men held their positions and continued blowing their trumpets. In the darkness, the Midianite soldiers could not recognize each other and began to fight one another with swords and spears. There was a mass slaughter as they killed their own soldiers on every side.

The remaining Midianite soldiers broke through Gideon's lines and began to flee down the Jezreel Valley. They ran and ran all night trying to escape.

Gideon needed more help, so he sent messengers throughout the northern tribes of Israel to help him fight the enemy. By dawn men from the tribes of Naphtali, Asher, Manasseh, and Ephraim were helping to pursue the Midianites.

"Stand guard at the Jordan River!" he commanded his soldiers. "Don't let the enemy escape across the river." Meanwhile, he and his men continued chasing what was left of the Midianite and Amalekite soldiers. Eventually they managed to capture two of their princes, Oreb and Zeeb, and two of their kings, Zebah and Zalmunna.

But not everyone helped Gideon fight the enemy as he had asked. In fact, some in the tribe of Ephraim were angry with him because they wanted to be the heroes instead of him. Some cities east of the Jordan refused to give him food

Grasping the torches in their left hands and holding the trumpets in their right hands, they shouted, "The sword of the Lord and of Gideon!"

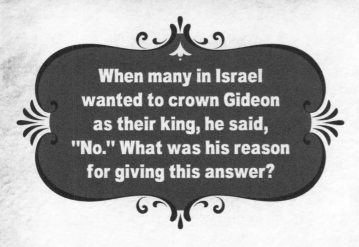

When many in Israel wanted to crown Gideon as their king, he said, "No." What was his reason for giving this answer?

for his men, who were exhausted from fighting so much.

But Gideon and his men kept chasing the enemy, and the Lord was with them. After a whole night and day of fighting the Midianites, they finally won the battle and gained a great victory.

When it was all over, the people were thankful that Gideon had helped them defeat the Midianites. They saw that he was a great leader and wanted to make him their king, but Gideon wouldn't allow it.

"I will not rule over you, nor shall my son rule over you," he told them. "The Lord is your King, and He will rule over you."

The Midianite raiders came no more to rob the Israelites. For 40 years, Israel continued to have peace, and all because Gideon had faith that God would help him do the impossible.

Talking with Jesus:

"Dear Father in heaven, help me to be brave for You like Gideon. Help me to be faithful to You, even though others might try to discourage me from doing right."

Samson and Delilah

This story is taken from Judges 16 and
Patriarchs and Prophets, chapter 54.

Samson, the strongest man in the Bible, was one of the weakest when it came to choosing a good women to fall in love with. For example, when Samson went down to the Valley of Sorek, he met a woman named Delilah. As you might know, that is one of the most famous stories in the whole Bible.

By now the Philistine rulers must have realized that if they were ever going to defeat Samson, they would have to discover the secret of his strength. And the perfect person to help them do it would be Delilah.

"If you can find out the secret of Samson's great strength, we will each pay you 1,100 pieces of silver," said the five lords of the Philistines.

Samson said, "If you weave the seven braids of my hair into the fabric on the loom, I'll become as weak as any other man."

So Delilah said to Samson, "Tell me the secret of your great strength and how you can be tied up and subdued."

Samson must have thought she was joking, because he gave her a foolish answer. "If anyone ties me with seven fresh bowstrings that have not been dried, I'll become as weak as any other man."

When Samson went to sleep that night, she followed his instructions and tied him up with the bowstrings. Then she shouted, "Samson, the Philistines are coming!" Not surprisingly, he jumped out of bed and snapped the bowstrings as if they were pieces of string, and the Philistine men who were hiding nearby waiting to kill him ran away.

Delilah acted as though she was hurt. "You have made a fool of me by lying to me," she pouted. "Tell me the truth. What is the secret of your strength?"

He must have laughed again, because he told her another tall tale about what she should do if she wanted him to be weak like other men. "If anyone ties me securely with new ropes that have never been used, I'll become as weak as other men."

Again Delilah followed his instructions, and again she failed, because when she woke him up he just snapped the ropes off his arms as if they were threads.

"Come on, Samson, tell me the truth!" she kept on pleading. "What is your secret?"

Samson was beginning to weaken now, but he didn't realize it. Closer and closer she was coming to the real source of his strength. "If you weave the seven braids of my hair into the fabric on the loom and tighten it with the pin, I'll become as weak as any other man," he said.

Delilah wasted no time. When he fell asleep she did just as he had said, but of course it

didn't work. When she shouted that the Philistines were coming, he awoke from his sleep and pulled up the pin and the loom with the fabric.

By now Delilah was getting desperate. If she failed, the Philistine rulers would be angry. "Please don't lie to me again!" she said, probably even shedding a few tears. "How can you say you love me when you keep lying to me? You've made a fool of me these three times, and still I don't know your secret!"

Day by day she nagged at him until he was sick of it. Finally he gave in and told her everything. "My hair has never been cut," he said, "because I have been a Nazirite dedicated to God from birth. If my head were ever to be shaved, my strength would leave me, and I would become as weak as any other man."

Delilah put Samson to sleep on her lap and called for someone to shave off the seven braids of his hair.

Delilah realized that Samson had told her the truth this time, so she sent for the Philistine lords. "He has told me everything," she said.

Then she put Samson to sleep on her lap and called for someone to shave off the seven braids of his hair. When the deed was done, she shouted as at other times, "Samson, the Philistines are coming!"

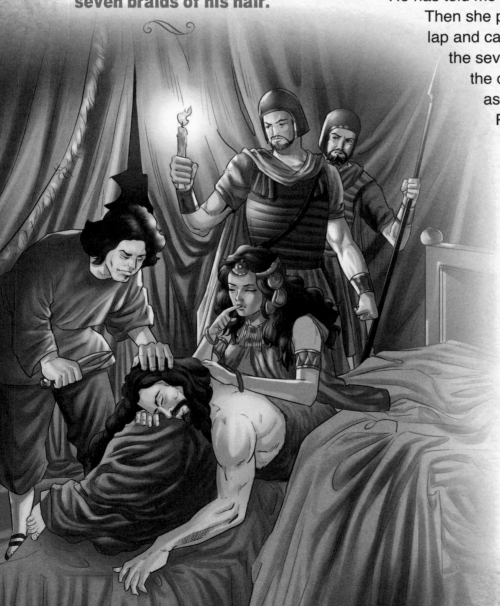

Samson awoke, but did not realize that his strength was gone until the Philistines attacked him. Quickly they tied him up, and then blinded him using a red-hot iron so he could never see again. They could have killed him, but they chose to keep him as a living trophy so they could make fun of him anytime they pleased.

Then they took him down to the fortress of Gaza, bound him with fetters, and put him to work grinding grain in the prison.

Samson knew he had failed God. He had been given an amazing gift of strength to be used for God's service, but he had used it only for himself selfishly. Now he must spend the rest of his days in a prison to be a laughingstock for anyone who came by to see him.

As the weeks and months went slowly by, he must have wished a thousand times that he had listened to his parents when they asked him to marry a girl from his own country. But his chances to make better choices were gone now forever.

And then slowly but surely Samson's hair began to grow back. He didn't really realize it at first, and the Philistines must not have thought about it either, but it was getting longer.

One day the Philistines gathered together in their temple to offer sacrifices to their god, Dagon, and to celebrate their good fortune at having captured Samson. "Our god has delivered Samson into our hands!" they sang and danced. "Once he was our enemy, but now he is our prisoner!"

When they were drunk and in high spirits, they called for Samson so they could mock him in his weakness.

A servant brought him into the temple, and Samson asked to be taken to the main pillars that supported the temple so he could lean on them.

By now the temple was crowded with people. All the rulers of the Philistines were there, and up on the roof were about 3,000 men and women who were enjoying the feast.

Samson spent the rest of his days in a prison to be a laughingstock for anyone who came by to see him.

How many times did Delilah try to weaken Samson?

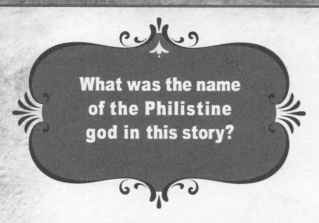

What was the name of the Philistine god in this story?

Samson prayed that God would forgive him for his past mistakes and his wasted life. And he also prayed for strength one more time to do what he knew must be done, though he knew it would end his life.

Then Samson put his hands against the two middle pillars on which the temple roof rested. Bracing himself with all his might, he broke the pillars, and the temple roof collapsed under its own weight. Samson died that day, but so did all the people worshipping in the pagan temple that day.

His death was a terrible blow to the Israelites, and it was a sad lesson learned for God's people for all time. The wages of sin is death, but if we obey God's commandments, we will live.

Samson braced himself with all his might, he broke the pillars, and the temple roof collapsed under its own weight.

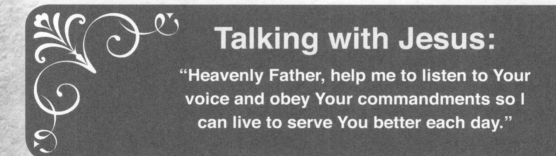

Talking with Jesus:

"Heavenly Father, help me to listen to Your voice and obey Your commandments so I can live to serve You better each day."

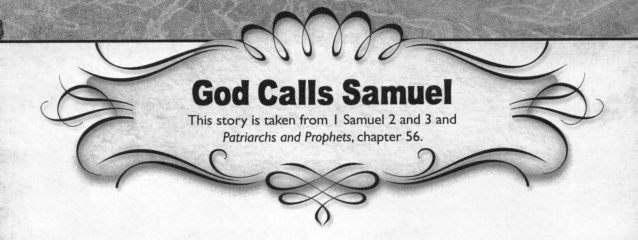

God Calls Samuel

This story is taken from 1 Samuel 2 and 3 and
Patriarchs and Prophets, chapter 56.

Samuel grew up at Shiloh learning all he could about the sacred ceremonies held at the sanctuary. There were the sacrifices to be offered, and those in themselves were almost a full-time job. Animals had to be inspected before they were killed at the altar. Some of the meat was to be put on the altar and a fire lit to burn the sacrifices as the Lord had directed. The leftover meat must then be divided between the priests and the family offering the sacrifice.

Of course, the priests had other responsibilities, such as offering prayers for the people and dedicating babies. And offerings had to be collected from the people, such as figs and pomegranates and grains such as wheat or barley.

But there were things the boy Samuel could do to help, and Eli put him to work right away doing simple tasks in the tabernacle sanctuary. Ashes had to be emptied from the altar for burnt offerings. Water needed to be brought for the priests to wash every day. Oil must be put in the seven-branched candlesticks, and the wicks had to be trimmed.

There were things Samuel could do to help, and Eli put him to work right away doing simple tasks in the tabernacle sanctuary.

He was such a helpful boy, and so obedient. It was such a wonderful change for Eli to have someone around whom he could depend on for all those odd jobs in the tabernacle. He had given up long ago trying to get help from his own boys, Hophni and Phinehas.

Growing up, they had been rascals of the worst sort, and Eli had not found it easy or convenient to make his boys mind. Because of this, he let them do whatever they wanted, whenever they wanted. He didn't stop to think that they would still be acting like that when they were old enough to help in the religious services at the sanctuary.

And that's exactly what happened. When Hophni and Phinehas grew up and Eli put them to work as priests in the sanctuary, they were an embarrassment to the family. This was a very bad thing for Israel, because his sons had no respect for God or the sacred services in which they now took part.

Soon they were doing all sorts of bad things at the sanctuary. For example, when families would bring their sacrifices to be offered at the tabernacle, Hophni and Phinehas

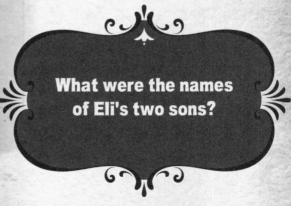

were not fair about how they divided up the meat. Some of it had to be offered on the altar as a sacrifice, but most of it was to be eaten by the family in a celebration meal. A small portion was to be given to the priests for food.

But Hophni and Phinehas would send their servants around to the worshippers at their campsites to take whatever they wanted. The leftover meat from the sacrifice would be boiling in a pot, and the servant would take much more than his share, caring little if there was any left at all for the family.

Also, Eli's sons would have wild parties where they feasted and drank wine with the women who served at the tabernacle gate. People who had come to worship the Lord knew that Hophni and Phinehas were doing these horrible things, and it made them angry. They knew that priests of the Lord should not be acting like that, but what could they do? Many became so discouraged that they stopped coming to worship the Lord in Shiloh at all.

Finally, Eli called his sons in and asked them, "Why do you do such things? Worshippers are telling me about all your wicked deeds. The rumors I hear are not good."

But Hophni and Phinehas wouldn't listen to him and kept on doing whatever they wanted.

Priest Eli should have put a stop to all this, but he didn't. He was very old now and was not able to control them. They had not respected him when they were boys, and now as adults they had no respect for him or God either.

Every year Hannah would make Samuel a little robe and bring it to him at Shiloh when she came to worship.

What were the names of Eli's two sons?

One day a man of God came to the tabernacle to give Eli some words of warning. "Your family has been honored to be priests of the Lord," he said, "but you have not been a good example to the people! Why do you abuse your privileges here at the sanctuary by stealing the best part of each sacrifice for you and your sons?

"God promised your family they would serve Him in the sanctuary forever, but now He has changed His mind! Soon He will punish you for the way you have treated Him here at His tabernacle!"

This prophecy made Eli very sad, but he wasn't shocked. He knew that he and his boys had been bad examples for the people of Israel.

Clearly Shiloh was not the best place for a young boy like Samuel to grow up, and yet even in these surroundings Samuel did well. His mother had raised him to love God and choose good over evil, and these things kept him faithful to God.

We can only imagine how much she must have missed him. Every year his mother would make him a little robe and bring it to him at Shiloh when she came to worship.

She must have been worried at the thought of having him live so near Hophni and Phinehas, but she trusted God to take care of her little son. After all, she had given him to the Lord.

One night as little Samuel was sleeping, he heard a voice calling him. Thinking Eli wanted him, Samuel jumped up and ran to the old man's bed. "I'm here," he said in the darkness. "What do you need?"

Eli shook his head. "I didn't call you. Go lie down."

Samuel was surprised, but he went back to his bed as he was told.

Three times the voice called him, and three times Samuel ran to Eli to find out what the old man needed.

One night as little Samuel was sleeping, he heard a voice calling him. Thinking Eli wanted him, Samuel jumped up and ran to him.

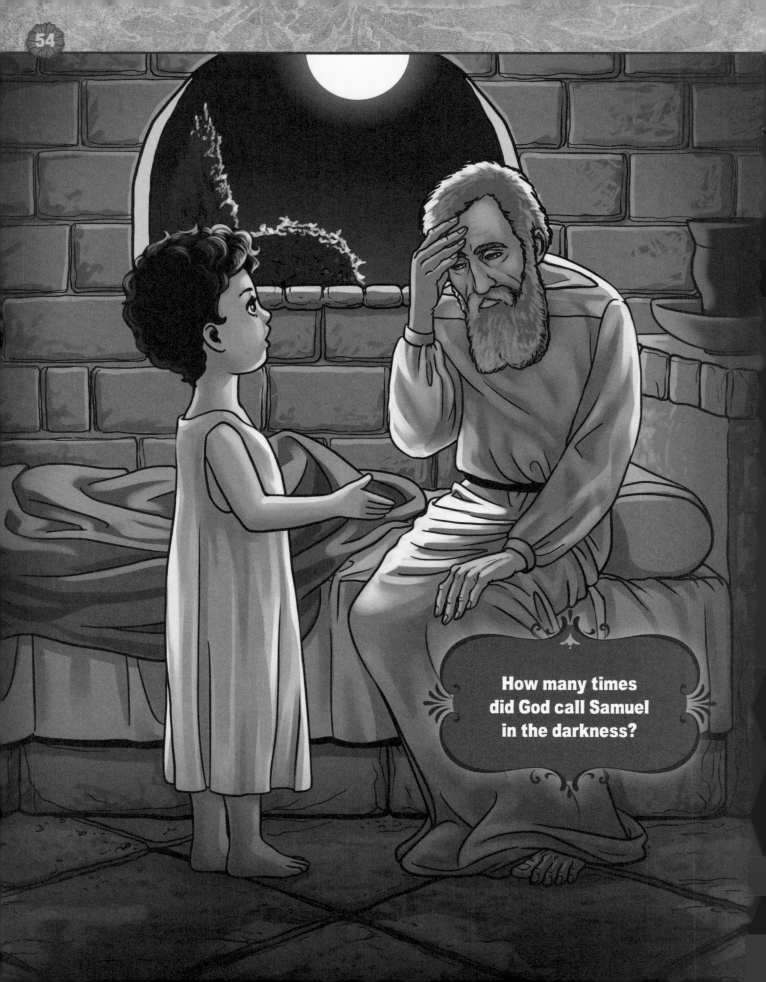

By now Eli knew it must be God who was trying to talk with Samuel. "Go and lie down," he told the boy, "and if the voice calls you again, just say, 'Speak, Lord, for Your servant is listening.'"

So Samuel went back to bed and waited. And, sure enough, the voice came again. "Samuel! Samuel!"

Samuel must have been so excited, and a little bit nervous, too. "Speak, for Your servant is listening" was all he remembered of the words Eli had told him to say.

Then it was that God told Samuel all He intended to do. It was a very serious message for a little boy to hear, but there was no one else in the Lord's house who would listen to the words of warning. "Judgment day for Eli cannot be stopped!" God said. "Because his sons have been so wicked, they are both going to die on the same day!"

The next morning Eli asked Samuel to tell him about the message God had given him the night before. We can see the little boy bowing his head to tell Eli the terrible message, but Eli was brave through it all. "The Lord is good," he said. "Let Him do what He thinks is best."

Three times the voice called him, and three times Samuel ran to Eli to find out what the old man needed.

Talking with Jesus:

"Dear Father in heaven, help me to listen to the voice of Your Holy Spirit when You call me."

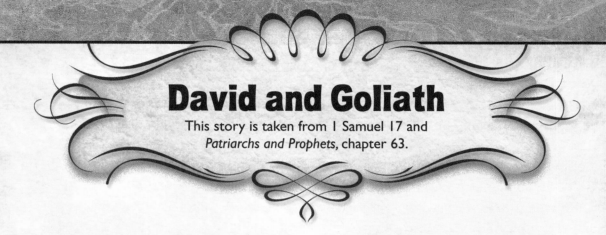

David and Goliath

This story is taken from 1 Samuel 17 and
Patriarchs and Prophets, chapter 63.

David stood at the top of a hill overlooking a huge valley below. He could see two camps of tents sprawled across the landscape. A small ravine with a creek in it ran down the center of the valley between the two camps. Crowds of men sat around early morning fires making their breakfasts.

"This must be the battlefield," David thought as he yanked on the donkey's lead rope. He could hardly wait to see his brothers. Unfortunately, the donkey had other ideas.

But if David thought his brothers would be glad to see him, he was wrong. "What are you doing here?" Eliab scowled when he saw David.

David was shocked at this reception. "I came to bring you food," he stammered in surprise. "The whole family is worried about you."

"You came to see the battle, that's all," Eliab growled. "We don't need you here! You're just a kid! Go home and take care of the sheep!"

David thought his brothers would be glad to see him. "I came to bring you food," he said.

Suddenly shouts rang out on the early morning air: "Here he comes!" And everybody started running toward the battlefield. David turned in time to see a giant soldier striding toward them from across the creek. The ground seemed to shake under the huge man's feet as he walked to the edge of the rocky ravine and shook his fist.

"King Saul!" The giant slapped his knee with one of his huge hands. "You are weak, and so is your God. Otherwise, you would have beaten us in battle long ago! I'm offering you the same chance I've given you for 40 days now! Send out your fiercest warrior to defeat me, and we will be your servants forever! However, if I beat my challenger, you must be our slaves." The Philistine soldiers in the front ranks broke into laughter.

David could hardly believe his eyes. This man was huge! He had heard of giants like this, but had never imagined one would look this big! With his helmet on, the hulk of a man looked to be half again as tall as any other man on the battlefield!

He was wearing a gigantic brass helmet, brass armor on his chest, and brass shin guards on his legs. The spear he was carrying was like a wooden beam with a humongous

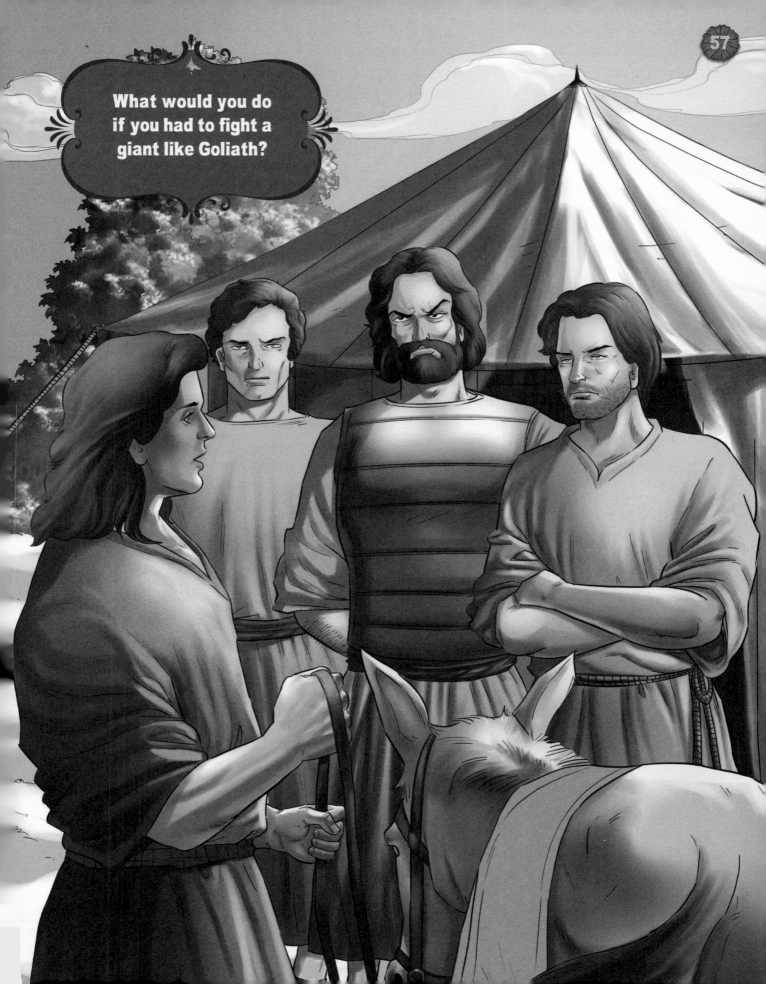

spearhead of iron, and the sword strapped at his side looked big enough to cut down a tree. And if that wasn't enough, out in front of the giant strode a fierce-looking warrior carrying a shield to protect him.

"I've never seen such a big man in my life!" David exclaimed. He couldn't take his eyes off the giant. "Who is he? Where's he from?"

"That's Goliath!" several Israelite soldiers shouted as they turned to run. "He's from the city of Gath down along the coast!"

"Where's everyone going?" David shouted. "You can't just run away! Isn't there someone brave enough to fight this man? He is cursing us and our God!"

A messenger ran to tell King Saul the brave words David had said, and soon David was being brought before the king. "Don't be afraid of this pagan giant," David assured the king. "Your servant will go and fight him."

David shouted, "Isn't there someone brave enough to fight this man? He is cursing our God!"

"You?" The king wanted to laugh, but he could see that David was perfectly serious. "How can you go? You're just a boy."

"I have fought my share of enemies," David said confidently. He told the king about his battles in the forests fighting lions, bears, and wolves to protect his sheep. "If I could kill those wild beasts, then God will help me beat this giant."

King Saul was amazed at David's faith and courage. He and his military commanders tried to convince David that fighting the giant was suicide, but David would have none of it. Finally, the king agreed to let David fight the giant, and he gave David his own armor to protect his body in battle.

But King Saul was a tall man, and the armor was far too big. "I can't wear these things," David admitted. "I would be in worse danger if I wore them because they don't fit." Then he walked off toward the battlefield with nothing but his shepherd's staff, his sling, and a leather pouch over his shoulder.

When he reached the edge of the ravine, Goliath was still there waiting to fight. When he caught sight of David, his face grew red with rage. In his rage he pushed up the helmet that protected his forehead.

"What is this!" he shouted angrily at the sight of the boy. "King Saul, you must think I'm a dog, or you wouldn't be sending a boy out to fight me. Look at him! He's carrying a stick!"

Goliath began to curse and swear as he swung his giant sword from side to side. "I'm going to get this over quickly," he shouted, "and then I will leave your body out on the field for the birds and wild animals to eat!"

David jumped down into the ravine and stepped into the water of the small creek. He kept his eye on the giant as he chose five smooth stones and put them into his pouch. Then he stood tall and faced the giant towering over him.

David kept his eye on the giant as he chose five smooth stones and put them into his pouch.

"You come to me with a sword and spear and javelin, Goliath, but I come to you in the name of the Lord of hosts, the Captain of the armies of heaven and earth!" David shouted loud enough for all the soldiers to hear. Then he pulled a stone from his pouch and slipped it into his sling. "Today my God will deliver you into my hand. But it isn't my strength or skill that will win this battle!" he added. "It will be the power of Jehovah, and then everyone will know that there is a God in Israel!"

Goliath couldn't stand David's words any longer and went crazy with rage! So when the Philistine arose and drew near to meet David, David hurried and ran toward the army to

meet the Philistine. A stone was already in his sling going around and around over David's head, and at just the right moment he let it go. The stone hit Goliath in the forehead with a whack. In the next instant, the giant came toppling down, and David wasted no time in running forward to kill Goliath with the man's own huge sword.

By now all was confusion on both sides of the ravine. The Israelite soldiers couldn't believe the outcome of the battle, and neither could the Philistines as they realized that their champion was dead. Suddenly the Philistine soldiers ran for their lives as they rushed back up over the hills toward their cities in the west.

David, the shepherd boy, had achieved a great victory for his people and his God! And it happened because he trusted in the Lord of hosts!

At just the right moment David let the stone go. Amazingly, the stone hit Goliath in the forehead.

Without faith in God and trusting Him to solve this "giant" problem, David would have never defeated Goliath. When you have problems in your life, even if they are problems as big as a giant, remember David. He prayed, and in faith tackled his giant problem, and the problem came tumbling down. So can yours.

Talking with Jesus:

"Help me, Lord, to be as brave as David when I have to face the giants in my life."

Healing Naaman

This story is taken from 2 Kings 5 and
Prophets and Kings, chapter 20.

Poor little girl! The Syrians had captured her from the land of Israel in a raid. She had been sold to the household of Naaman, who was commander of King Ben-Hadad's army in Damascus. We don't know her name, for the Bible simply calls her "little maiden" or "little maid." We can imagine that she was very frightened to be living as a slave in a foreign country. She must have been very homesick, too. However, it is clear that she loved God and trusted that He would be with her, even in Damascus, where no one worshipped Jehovah, the one true God.

One day the little maid found out that Captain Naaman was very sick. His sickness couldn't be cured, and it was the worst of all diseases. He had leprosy, the dreaded, deadly skin disease, and it made him an outcast, even among his own people.

"If Captain Naaman wants to be healed, he should go to the prophet Elisha in Israel," the little maid told Naaman's wife, whom she served. "Prophet Elisha has done many mighty miracles, and I'm sure he could help your husband."

When Captain Naaman's wife told him what the servant girl had said, he must have believed, because he went to King Ben-Hadad immediately. He said, "I would like to go to Samaria in Israel to receive healing for my leprosy."

"If Captain Naaman wants to be healed, he should go to the prophet Elisha in Israel."

So he made the journey, taking with him a letter from King Ben-Hadad asking that the king of Israel arrange for Naaman to be healed of his leprosy. He took with him payment for his healing: 10 talents of silver, 6,000 shekels of gold, and 10 sets of clothing. Would that be worth a lot today? Absolutely! In today's money, it would total more than a million dollars!

"He wants me to do what?" we can hear Israel's King Joram shouting in his throne room, as he read the contents of the letter. "King Ben-Hadad is asking that I cure Captain Naaman of his leprosy!" The king tore his clothes, which was the custom when one was very sad or upset. "Am I God that I can do such a thing? Look! King Ben-Hadad wants to

start a war between our countries, and how does he do it? By asking me to heal his highest-ranking general of leprosy!"

The whole thing could have become quite a disaster, but when Elisha heard about it, he quickly sent a message to the royal palace. "Why are you so upset?" he asked the king. "Ask the captain to come see me. Then he will know that there is a God in Israel, and that I am His prophet."

Naaman and his company of soldiers left immediately for Elisha's house. However, when they arrived, a servant came out to greet them with a simple message. "Go and dip yourself in the Jordan seven times. Do this, and your skin will be healed."

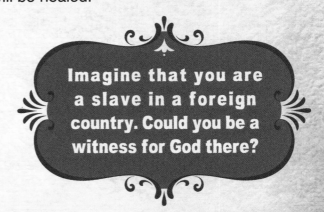

Imagine that you are a slave in a foreign country. Could you be a witness for God there?

"Go, dip yourself in the Jordan seven times. Do this, and your skin will be healed."

Captain Naaman could hardly believe his ears. "Wash in the Jordan River! I think not!" he raged. "Aren't the rivers of Damascus better than all the rivers in Israel? Can't I wash in them and be healed?" He turned away in disgust. "I thought at least the prophet would come out to me and call on the Lord his God. I thought maybe he would wave his hand over the spot and cure me of my leprosy that way. Now he insults me with a command like this! Go wash in the Jordan, indeed!"

In anger and pride, Captain Naaman jumped into his chariot to begin the journey back to Damascus. "Let's get out of here! I knew it was too good to be true," he yelled. "Let's go. We've still got some daylight to travel."

His advisers and attendants went after him. As they rode up close beside him, they respectfully and fearfully appealed to him, saying, "If the prophet had told you to do something really difficult, wouldn't you have done it? Why not do this simple thing!"

Naaman slowed his chariot to a crawl, his mind deep in thought. "You're right," he finally admitted. "I guess I need to set aside my pride." Without further argument, he turned his chariot around and headed for the Jordan.

The spots were gone! His skin was as new...

Soon he was standing on its banks, staring at the waters of the muddy river.

He waded in until he was waist-deep, and then dipped himself under the water. But when he came up, there was no change to his skin. The leprosy was still as obvious as ever.

Captain Naaman dipped into the water again and stared at his arms and chest. The white spots were still on him, and he frowned.

"Keep going!" his men cheered him on. "He told you seven times."

Naaman dipped himself in the water a third time and then a fourth. Five times, six times, seven times. When he came up the seventh time, his mouth dropped open in surprise, and his eyes grew wide in astonishment! The spots were gone! His skin was as new and fresh as that of a young boy! "I'm healed!" he shouted excitedly as he ran splashing out of the river. "I'm healed! My leprosy is gone!" He threw on his clothes, jumped into his chariot, and raced up the road to Elisha's house. Can you imagine how the dust flew on that country road? Surely the angels must have smiled at God's goodness. A pagan man who knew nothing of heaven's bountiful gifts had just received healing, the greatest of all gifts, and all because he had stepped forward in faith.

"Keep your gifts. God gives life to all who ask, and healing to those who have faith."

When Naaman reached the prophet's house, Elisha was waiting for him. Captain Naaman jumped down from the chariot and knelt with his face to the ground. "Now I know that there is no God in all the earth but in Israel.

Thank you, thank you!" he exclaimed as he knelt before the prophet. Tears streamed down his face as he realized just how blessed he was. And to think that he almost went home, too proud to obey the prophet, who held the only hope for the healing of his leprosy!

What wonderful things has God done for you that you can share with others?

"And now I have a few gifts for you," he said with the biggest smile on his face. "Please accept them, though they cannot really pay for the life you have given me back today."

Elisha smiled too, but he held up his hand. "Keep your gifts. The Lord my God gives life to all who ask, and healing to those who have faith. He wishes for no more than your heart in worship. Do this, and you shall have eternal life in Him." Naaman went home a changed man, thanks to a little girl who shared her faith.

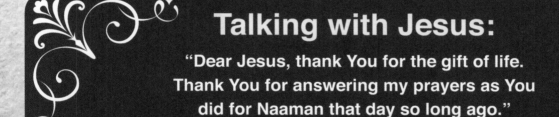

Talking with Jesus:

"Dear Jesus, thank You for the gift of life. Thank You for answering my prayers as You did for Naaman that day so long ago."

Jonah and the Whale

This story is taken from Jonah 1-4 and
Prophets and Kings, chapter 22.

One of the most famous stories in the Bible is about Jonah and the whale. Jonah was a prophet who lived in Israel about 800 years before Jesus. He lived during a time when most people no longer worshipped the God of heaven. God spoke to Jonah, telling him, "Arise, go to Nineveh, that great city, and cry out against it, for their wickedness has come up before Me."

But Jonah didn't want to go to Nineveh, and he tried to flee from the presence of the Lord. He did this by fleeing to Joppa, where he found a ship going in the opposite direction of Nineveh. There he paid his fare and went down into the ship to hide from God.

Jonah didn't want to go to Nineveh, and he tried to flee from the presence of the Lord. He did this by fleeing to Joppa.

Jonah's ship had not been at sea very long when a violent storm came up. The Bible says that the Lord sent a great wind and a mighty tempest on the sea so that the ship was about to be broken up.

The sailors were all afraid, and each man prayed frantically to his god, but the storm only got worse. Soon the sailors began throwing the ship's cargo into the sea to lighten the load. However, Jonah knew nothing about the storm. He was down in the lower levels of the ship fast asleep.

How anyone could sleep in a storm such as that is a wonder, but that is where the ship's captain found him. "What are you doing, sleeper?" he demanded when he woke him up. "Arise, call on your God; perhaps your God will consider us, so that we may not perish."

The sailors were all very superstitious and finally said, "Come, let us cast lots that we may know for whose cause this trouble has come upon us." There were many ways to cast lots in those days. Sometimes they drew straws, with the shortest straw showing who was the guilty one.

That is what they did. The lot fell on Jonah. God arranged for Jonah to get the "shortest straw" so the sailors would know that Jonah was running away from God. Then they would

The men picked Jonah up and threw him into the sea, and immediately the sea calmed down.

learn that God was the Creator of heaven and earth and that He was in control of everything, including the weather.

Everyone was frightened now. "Please tell us!" they demanded. "What is your occupation, and where do you come from? What is your country, and who are your people?"

"I am a Hebrew," Jonah said. "I fear the Lord, the God of heaven who made the sea and the dry land."

When Jonah told them that he was running away from God, the sailors were really scared. "Why have you done this?" they said. "What shall we do that the sea may be calm for us?"

Jonah told them, "Pick me up and throw me into the sea; then the sea will become calm for you. For I know that this great storm is because of me."

However, the men didn't want to do that, so they rowed even harder to return to land. But the storm was so bad that it was impossible. Then they cried out to the Lord, "We pray, O Lord, please do not let us perish for this man's life, and do not charge us with innocent blood." Then they picked Jonah up and threw him into the sea, and immediately the sea calmed down. When the sailors saw this, they greatly feared the Lord and offered a sacrifice to Him.

Jonah was sure he would drown in the sea, but God was watching out for him. As he was sinking into the ocean

Where did the captain of the ship find Jonah sleeping during the storm?

waters, the Lord prepared a big fish to swallow him. For three days, Jonah was in the belly of that fish. He prayed that God would save him. "I have been cast out of Your sight," he prayed. "Yet I will look again toward Your holy temple. The waters surrounded me, even to my soul. The deep closed around me, and weeds were wrapped around my head. Yet You have brought up my life from the pit, O Lord, my God. I will sacrifice to You with the voice of thanksgiving. I will pay what I have vowed. Salvation is of the Lord."

Then God heard Jonah's prayer, and He spoke to the fish so that it vomited Jonah onto the dry land.

God spoke to Jonah the second time. "Arise, go to Nineveh, that great city, and preach to it the message that I tell you."

Jonah didn't hesitate this time to do as God asked him. He immediately set out for Nineveh. When Jonah reached the city, it took him three days to walk through its streets, and his message to the people was a serious

Jonah's message to the people was a serious one. "In 40 days, Nineveh shall be overthrown!"

one. "In 40 days, Nineveh shall be overthrown!"

The king of Nineveh was very upset when he heard Jonah's message, and he believed him. The king came down from his throne and laid aside his royal robes to put on sackcloth and ashes as if he were in mourning.

Then he ordered by royal decree that everyone in Nineveh should follow his example, from the greatest to the least of them. "Let everyone turn from his evil way!" he said. "Who can tell if God will turn away from His fierce anger so that we may not perish?"

Sure enough, when God saw that the king and his subjects repented and turned from their wicked ways, He decided not to punish the city.

But Jonah was not happy about this at all. "Was not this what I said would happen when I was still in my country?" he said to God. "Therefore I tried to flee to Tarshish, for I know that You are a gracious and merciful God, slow to anger, and abundant in lovingkindness."

So Jonah went out of the city and made a little shelter to sit under in the shade. And God made a little plant grow up that day so it could give

Jonah was very hot under the sun and was angry about the plant withering.

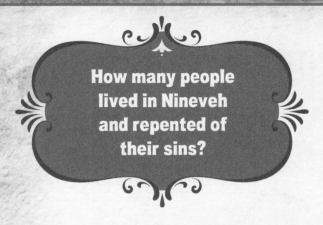

How many people lived in Nineveh and repented of their sins?

Jonah some shade to keep him cool. Jonah was grateful to God for the plant, but the next morning a worm chewed on the plant stem and the plant withered. Jonah was very hot under the sun and was angry about the plant withering.

"You care more about the plant than you do the city," God scolded Jonah. "Shouldn't I also pity Nineveh, that great city, in which are more than 120,000 people who cannot discern between their right hand and their left?"

The message that we can all take from this great story is that God knows what He is doing. When He tells us something, we should do it the first time.

The same is true with being obedient to our parents. If we do what we are told the first time, things will be much better and everyone will be a lot happier.

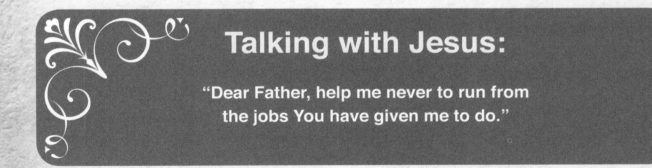

Talking with Jesus:

"Dear Father, help me never to run from the jobs You have given me to do."

The Fiery Furnace

This story is taken from Daniel 3 and
Prophets and Kings, chapter 41.

The day was a hot one. Thousands of government officials from every province had gathered on the plain of Dura to celebrate King Nebuchadnezzar's latest creation. There it stood, 90 feet tall, made of gleaming, shining gold.

"Good people from every nation and language," a royal crier announced, "when you hear the sound of the horn, flute, harp, lyre, and psaltery, in symphony with all kinds of music, you shall fall down and worship the golden image that King Nebuchadnezzar has set up."

The crier pointed to a group of brick kilns behind the golden statue. "And whoever does not fall down and worship shall be cast immediately into the midst of a burning, fiery furnace."

All fell flat on their faces except three young officials way out in the middle of the assembly.

A gasp of terror went up from the crowd at this announcement, as many dropped to their knees in fear. Then, as the shrill notes of the instruments hit the morning air, the huge crowd fell flat on their faces to the ground in worship of the golden image.

All, that is, except three young officials way out in the middle of the assembly. They weren't bowing on their faces to the ground in honor of the gods. In fact, they weren't even on their knees.

"Oh, king, live forever!" A group of Chaldean officials stepped forward, no doubt hoping to score points with the king. "There are certain Jews whom you have honored and set over the affairs of the province of Babylon: Shadrach, Meshach, and Abed-Nego by name. They do not serve your gods or worship the golden image which you have set up."

The king was angry, and in fury gave the command, "Bring them to me!"

The soldiers went at once, and soon they returned with Shadrach, Meshach, and Abed-Nego to stand before the king. He asked them, "Is it true, Shadrach, Meshach, and Abed-Nego, that you do not serve my gods or worship the gold image which I have set up?"

Shadrach, Meshach, and Abed-Nego answered, "What they say is true, your majesty. We did not worship as you commanded."

"But why?" There must have been a look of surprise and confusion on the king's face. "If you fall down and worship the image which I have made, that's good! But if you do not worship, you shall be cast immediately into the midst of a burning, fiery furnace. And who is the god that will deliver you from my hands? Let's begin again," he probably added, staring at the three handsome young men standing before him.

> **How tall was Nebuchadnezzar's golden image?**

"Oh, Nebuchadnezzar," the three young men bowed their heads respectfully, "we have no need to answer you in this matter. Our God whom we serve is able to deliver us from the burning, fiery furnace, and He will deliver us from your hand, oh, king. But if not, let it be known to you, oh, king, that we will not serve your gods, nor will we worship the golden image that you have set up."

At this, King Nebuchadnezzar's face grew dark, and his smile vanished. "Oh, really! So that's the way you want it!" we can almost hear him snarling, and the veins in his neck began popping out. "Fine! We will just see what we can do about that!" he roared to his attendants as he stood to his feet. "Heat up that furnace! Make it seven times hotter than usual! I'll teach these boys to fool with me!"

Guards immediately seized Shadrach, Meshach, and Abed-Nego and bound them hand and foot with strong ropes. Workers at the kiln furnace began throwing in more fuel.

"Carry these ungrateful wretches to the furnace and throw them in!" the king shouted to his burly bodyguards. "They will not escape my wrath! We will put a stop to this nonsense about their God once and for all!"

Shadrach, Meshach, and Abed-Nego were dragged to the edge of the field and up the steps to the dome-shaped furnace. Roaring flames and billowing smoke could be seen pouring from the stack as workers continued stoking the furnace.

The bodyguards got as near as they could to throw the boys in, but as they did, the heat from the furnace was so intense that the guards died. Shadrach, Meshach, and Abed-Nego fell into the flames and landed in a heap on the floor of the fiery furnace.

King Nebuchadnezzar could see the open door of the furnace. As he peered into the flames, to his surprise he saw the three young men getting to their feet again. They even began walking around, but the ropes on their hands and feet were now gone. The fire had burned them off.

The king was astonished and ran down the steps from his throne toward the furnaces. He squinted hard into the burning inferno. "Wait a minute!" And he stepped even closer to the blistering heat coming from the open doorway to the furnace. "Didn't we throw three men bound into the fire? Look! I see four men loose, walking in the midst of the fire. They are not hurt, and the form of the fourth is like the Son of God."

Nebuchadnezzar had once again been introduced to the God of heaven and earth. Through his friendship with Shadrach, Meshach, and Abed-Nego, and by their godly example, he had seen the character of God in their lives. When he saw the Lord in the fiery furnace, he recognized Him as the Son of God.

Everyone was speechless at the sight before them, but the king shouted, "Shadrach, Meshach, and Abed-Nego, servants of the most high God, come out!"

The three young men then stepped from the searing heat of the flames, and as they did, the mysterious fourth Man disappeared.

The king rushed forward to greet Shadrach, Meshach, and Abed-Nego. He grabbed their hands and examined them for burns! He touched their faces to feel their eyebrows and beards, but not a hair had been singed in the flames. He even smelled their robes and turbans, but not a trace of smoke could he detect.

Then the king humbly dropped to his knees before the boys and put his face to the ground. "Blessed be the God of Shadrach, Meshach, and Abed-Nego,

"Didn't we throw three men bound into the fire? Look! I see four men loose."

who sent His Angel and rescued His servants, because they were willing to surrender their lives rather than worship any god except Jehovah. From this day forward all people of every nation and language shall pay homage to this God, for no other god can save in this way."

It was true. Shadrach, Meshach, and Abed-Nego had been faithful to the one true God, and

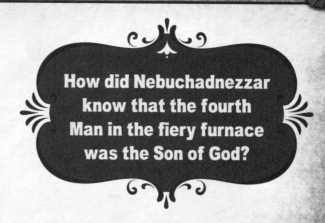

How did Nebuchadnezzar know that the fourth Man in the fiery furnace was the Son of God?

He had brought them through the flames untouched. The evidence could not be denied! Now thousands who had seen the miracle would go home to their own countries and tell this amazing story. They would tell everyone that the God of heaven is so powerful that He can keep a fiery furnace from hurting His people. Shadrach, Meshach, and Abed-Nego were living proof of it!

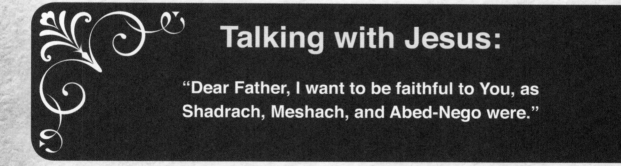

Talking with Jesus:

"Dear Father, I want to be faithful to You, as Shadrach, Meshach, and Abed-Nego were."

In the Lions' Den

This story is taken from Daniel 6 and
Prophets and Kings, chapter 44.

When the Babylonian Empire was overthrown by the Medo-Persians, Darius the Mede was made king. In his new government, he set up 120 officials called satraps to be over all the provinces of the kingdom. Three governors were put above them all, and Daniel was chosen as prime minister because he had been such a good administrator in Babylon.

He did very well in his new position and distinguished himself above all the other government leaders. This made the other officers extremely jealous, and they tried to find some fault in him so they could have him overthrown. However, try as they might, they could not find anything with which to convict him. He was so faithful in his duties, and he never made a mistake.

"Whoever prays to any god or man for 30 days, except you, O king, shall be cast into the den of lions." King Darius liked the idea of such a decree and signed it immediately.

Finally, the conspirators said to one another, "We shall not find any charge against this Daniel unless we find it against him concerning the law of his God."

So these governors and satraps came before King Darius and said, "All the government leaders would like to propose a new decree. Whoever prays to any god or man for 30 days, except you, O king, shall be cast into the den of lions. We have that decree ready for you to sign and seal with your ring today so that it cannot be changed, according to the law of the Medes and Persians."

King Darius liked the idea of such a decree and signed it immediately. Unfortunately, he was a proud, vain man, so he never suspected that his government leaders would plan such a thing to get rid of Daniel. But it was true, and the results of his new decree came sooner than he would have thought possible.

Daniel saw the decree and knew that it was already signed, but decided he would pray to God anyway. That was his daily habit, and he was not about to sacrifice his loyalty to God just because someone wanted him killed.

Daniel saw the decree and knew that it was already signed, but decided he would pray to God anyway. That was his daily habit.

So he went to an upper room in his palace apartment with his windows open toward Jerusalem. There he knelt three times that day to pray and give thanks to God, as he had always done since he was a young man.

But the government officers were spying on him and found him in the act of praying. Three times he prayed, and when the day was over, they went before the king, saying, "Daniel, a captive from the land of Judah, does not show respect to you, O king. He has not obeyed the decree you have signed, but makes petition to his God three times a day."

When the king heard these words, he knew that he had been tricked. He tried everything he could to overturn the law, but once a law of the Medes and Persians was signed, it could not be changed.

And so it was with great sadness that the king called for Daniel, and he was taken to the den of lions to be thrown to the wild beasts. The king probably wept some very bitter tears as he thought about how he had allowed his pride to overcome his common sense.

However, he had one glimmer of hope even now. As he threw Daniel to the lions, he said with a faith that he could have learned only from Daniel, "Your God, whom you serve continually, He will deliver you."

Then they brought a large stone, laid it over the mouth of the den, and set a royal seal on it.

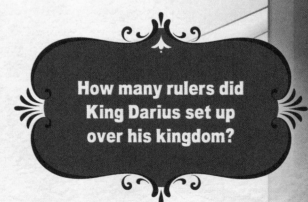

How many rulers did King Darius set up over his kingdom?

The king was so worried about Daniel and felt so guilty about what he had done that he could not sleep all night.

Early the next morning he got up and hurried out to the den of lions. He looked into the deep, dark pit and yelled, "Daniel, servant of the living God, has your God, whom you serve continually, been able to deliver you from the lions?" He was hoping that Daniel's God was as powerful as Daniel had told him He was.

What new decree did the king sign?

The king didn't have to wait long for his friend to answer. "O king, live forever!" came back Daniel's confident reply. "My God sent His angel and shut the lions' mouths, so that they have not hurt me because I was found innocent before Him; and also, O king, I have done no wrong before you."

The king was so happy that Daniel was still alive and commanded that he be taken out of the den of lions. However, he was still very angry with the government officers who had tricked and conspired against him. And now he called for all those men and brought them to the lions' den and threw them to the wild beasts.

Then they brought a large stone, laid it over the mouth of the den, and set a royal seal on it.

Then the king made a new decree: "In every dominion of my kingdom men must tremble and fear before the God of Daniel, for He is the living God! He works signs and wonders in heaven and on earth, who has delivered Daniel from the power of the lions."

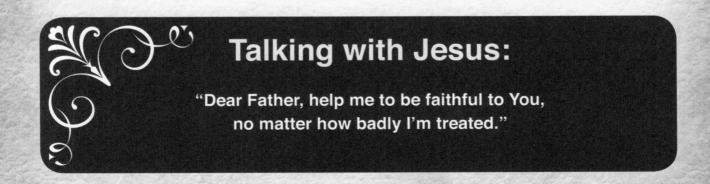

Talking with Jesus:

"Dear Father, help me to be faithful to You, no matter how badly I'm treated."

Beauty Queen

This story is taken from Esther 2-5 and
Prophets and Kings, chapter 49.

Hadassah was an orphan child in a nation of Jews who had been living in Babylon and Persia since the days of Daniel. At an early age, she lost her parents and came to live with her cousin Mordecai in the royal city of Shushan. He became a father to her and taught her to love Jehovah, the one true God.

From Mordecai, she learned the sacred stories of her people. Stories about Noah, Abraham, and Moses reminded her that God would care for His people. He would answer their prayers if they called on Him in the time of need. Some stories made her laugh, such as the one about the frogs in Egypt and the one about Balaam's talking donkey. There were always lessons from the stories, such as learning to trust God or being brave enough to stand up for the right.

At an early age, Hadassah lost her parents and came to live with her cousin Mordecai in the royal city of Shushan.

While still a young maiden, Hadassah became famous for her incredible beauty. When King Ahasuerus, also known as Xerxes, announced a national beauty contest to choose a new queen for the empire, Hadassah was chosen as one of the finalists.

For 12 months, she went through a series of beauty treatments in preparation for the beauty contest. Hegai, the court adviser in charge of the beauty contestants, found Hadassah to be a wonderful young woman, simple in her tastes, and humble in every way. Everyone in the royal palace fell in love with the gorgeous girl, including the king.

When the king chose her to be the next queen, Hadassah was surprised. Hadassah had not told anyone that she was Jewish. Following the advice of Mordecai, she disguised her identity with the Persian name "Esther." But could she keep her secret and still remain faithful to the God of her fathers? Time would tell.

Mordecai was a scribe in the royal palace, and as fate would have it, he somehow uncovered a royal assassination plot. He learned that Bigthan and Teresh, two of the bodyguards who guarded the private chambers of the king, had, in fact, decided to kill him. Mordecai relayed the information to Esther, and she reported it to the king. The bodyguards

were quickly arrested and then executed. The part Mordecai played in the arrest of the bodyguards had saved King Ahasuerus' life, but for some reason the good deed went unrewarded.

Not long after this, King Ahasuerus promoted Haman, who was one of his special advisers, to become the next prime minister of Persia. Haman was a proud man who loved to have people bow to him as he went about the king's business in the palace.

However, Mordecai did not think it right that one man should demand the worship of another. Jews worshipped only the God of heaven. He knew that Haman was a powerful man, but he still refused to give the honor that belonged to God alone to the prime minister.

When the king chose her to be the next queen, Hadassah was surprised.

Haman was furious at being snubbed by a man of lower rank and vowed that he would get even. He would see that Mordecai was destroyed one way or another. When he realized that Mordecai was a Jew, he hatched an even more evil plan. He thought, "Why not arrange for Mordecai to be executed and all his people as well?"

Skillfully, he wrote a proposal advising the king to search out and destroy a certain race of people in his kingdom who were lawless and evil. "To pay for this war, I will give 10,000 talents of silver from my own treasury!" Haman promised. "The plunder we get from the cities and homes of our victims will be more than enough to pay me back!" Of course, he did not reveal which race of people he would target, but the king didn't ask and foolishly agreed to sign Haman's decree anyway.

The king would not find out until later exactly whom the decree was written for, but by then it was too late. The laws of the Persian court could not be reversed once they had been signed and sealed with the king's signet ring.

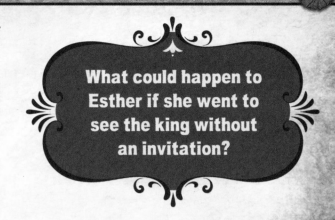

What could happen to Esther if she went to see the king without an invitation?

Almost immediately, dispatchers were sent by couriers to every province in the kingdom with orders to destroy all the Jews and to plunder their property. All of this was to take place on a single day, which was the 13th day of the 12th month.

When Mordecai saw a copy of the new decree posted, he dressed himself in sackcloth and began to weep and wail as though he was already mourning for the dead to come.

Queen Esther heard of Mordecai's protest and sent a messenger to him.

The messenger returned to Esther with a letter from Mordecai along with a copy of the decree. "Our people are doomed to a terrible death," he wrote. "You must go to the king and plead with him on our behalf!"

Back came Esther's reply to Mordecai. "I cannot approach the king without an invitation. It is against Persian law. I could die if I did such a thing."

"Do not think that you will escape death just because you live in the royal palace," Mordecai was persistent. "God Himself will be your judge. If you do not come to the rescue of Jews everywhere, the blood of our people will be on your hands. And who knows," he added, "it could be that God has brought you to the royal palace for just such a time as this."

"You're right," Esther wrote back humbly. "Go, gather together all the Jews who are in Shushan, and fast for me. I and my attendants will fast as you do. When this is done, I will go to the king, even though it is against the law. And if I perish, I perish."

The days of fasting passed all too quickly, and on the third day Esther went to the royal throne room. She wore her best robes and her finest perfumes, but in her heart was a prayer to God that He touch the king's heart.

When the king saw Queen Esther standing in the court, he stretched out his scepter and accepted her into his presence. "What is your wish?" he asked. "You may have anything you desire up to half of my kingdom."

"I would like very much for you to come to a banquet in my quarters this afternoon," Esther said sweetly. "And bring Haman, the prime minister, along, too," she added. Her face was calm, but her heart must have been beating wildly. At that banquet, she knew she was going to have to tell the king that Haman was planning to destroy her and her people.

Queen Esther invited the king to a banquet, and Haman, the prime minister, came as a guest of honor, too. They enjoyed a delicious meal, and again the king asked what Esther desired of him. She could have anything she wanted, he said.

Queen Esther invited the king and Haman to come again the next day for another banquet. Instead of telling the king about Haman's evil plans right then, she decided to wait another day.

When the king saw Queen Esther standing in the court, he stretched out his scepter and accepted her into his presence.

Haman was very excited that he had been invited to dine with the king and queen, and the fact that he was the only guest made it an even greater honor. However, on his way out of the banquet hall, he met Mordecai. Unfortunately for Haman, Mordecai again refused to bow as he passed in the hallway.

This made Haman furious, but he held his tongue. After all, he had just come from a royal banquet with the king and queen. However, when he got home he called together his family and friends and told them what had happened.

"I am probably the wealthiest man in Shushan," Haman growled. "I have many sons, and the king has promoted me above all the nobles and officials in his kingdom. I was the only guest invited by Queen Esther to dine

Queen Esther invited the king to a banquet, and Haman, the prime minister, came as a guest of honor, too. The king asked what Esther desired of him.

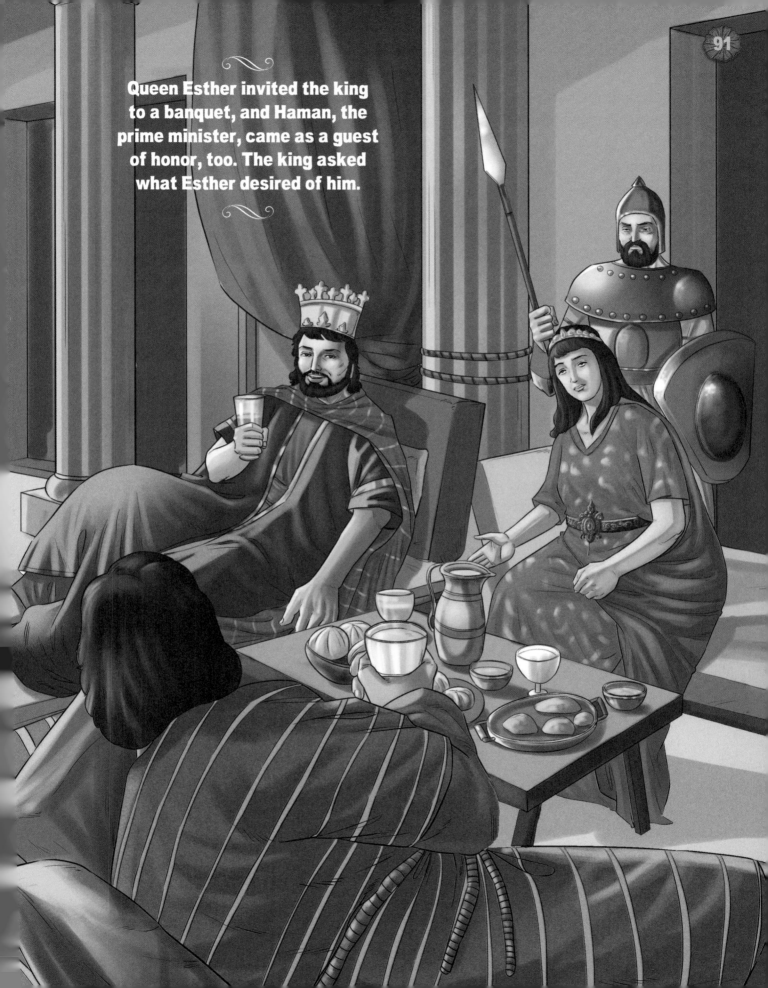

with her and the king this afternoon. Besides all this, she has invited me to come to another banquet tomorrow. But all of this gives me no satisfaction as long as I see that worthless Jew, Mordecai, sitting at the king's gate!" he thundered.

"If you don't like him, get rid of him," Haman's wife said. "After all, you are the prime minister."

"That's right!" his friends added. "And you should make it a public thing! Set up a pole at least 75 feet tall, and then in the morning ask the king to have Mordecai hung on that pole to die. Then go with the king to the banquet and enjoy yourself."

Haman liked the idea, and he ordered that the pole be set up.

"If I have found favor with you, O king, my petition is that you spare me and my people, for we have all been condemned to die."

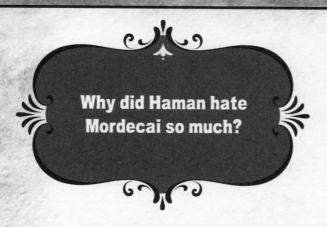

Why did Haman hate Mordecai so much?

That night the king had a hard time sleeping, so he asked for some entertainment. His attendants suggested bringing in the books of the royal chronicles so they could read to him all the things that had happened during his reign. While reading, they found the report that Mordecai had uncovered the plot in which King Ahasuerus' two bodyguards planned to assassinate him.

"What honor and recognition has Mordecai received for this?" the king asked in surprise.

"Nothing has been done for him," his attendants answered.

By now, it was morning and Haman had arrived at the royal court. The king called him into his private chambers. "What should be done for the man whom I want to honor?" he asked.

Haman thought to himself vainly, "Who else but me could the king want to honor?" So he said, "If you wish to honor a man, bring a royal robe that the king has worn, and a horse that the king has ridden with a royal crest placed on its head. Then let the robe and horse be entrusted to one of the king's most noble princes. Take the man the king delights to honor and lead him on the horse through the city streets announcing, 'This is what should be done for the man the king wishes to honor!'"

"Excellent idea! Go at once!" the king commanded Haman. "Get the robe and the horse and do just as you have suggested for Mordecai the Jew, who sits at the palace gate. Don't leave a thing out that you have recommended."

Haman was horrified and very upset. He didn't want to follow the king's orders, but he had to.

Now, of course, he dared not let the king know about his plans to execute Mordecai! That would be suicide! Right now, circumstances were quickly getting out of hand. But if Haman thought things were going badly now, he was in for a real shocker!

The next few hours were very humiliating for Haman. He got the king's horse and put King Ahasuerus' most elaborate robes on Mordecai. Then he paraded Mordecai on horseback down the street from the royal palace. "This is what is done for the man that the king delights to honor!" he shouted loudly to the crowds as he passed.

After the procession returned to the gates of the palace, Haman hurried home to hide his shame. The night before he had come home angry and arrogant. Tonight he walked with his head covered in disgrace. "Mordecai is the talk of the town," he moaned, "and I have been made the biggest fool!" He told the whole story, but his wife and friends weren't much help.

"This is bad news!" they all said. "You cannot stand against Mordecai now that he has been honored by the king. This may be the beginning of the end for you."

And if that was not bad enough news for him, while they were still talking the king's messengers arrived and took Haman away to Esther's royal banquet.

King Ahasuerus' face grew red with rage. "Take him!" he growled, pointing at Haman. "Execute him on his own gallows!"

Haman was not in a good mood at the banquet, but he tried to hide his feelings. While they dined, the king asked the question on everybody's mind. "Queen Esther, what is your petition? Ask what you want, and it will be granted you, even up to half of my kingdom."

Esther knew that she could wait no longer to make her wishes known to the king. "If I have found favor with you, O king, my petition is that you spare me and my people, for we have all been condemned to die."

King Ahasuerus was stunned. "Who would dare to do such a thing?"

Esther pointed at Haman. "The adversary and enemy is this wicked Haman!"

The king could not believe it! He was furious and began to pace the royal gardens next to the banquet hall.

Haman was in a panic. "Please, Queen Esther," he begged, "there has been a horrible mistake!"

"Look, your majesty!" A bodyguard pointed out the window to

Whom did Esther invite to her banquet twice?

Haman's execution pole. "Haman built those gallows to order Mordecai's death, the scribe who uncovered the plot of those who tried to assassinate you!"

King Ahasuerus' face grew red with rage. "Take him!" he growled, pointing at Haman. "Execute him on his own gallows!" And that is exactly what they did.

The king then wrote a new decree. He could not overturn the decree that Haman had already written, because the laws of the Persians did not allow for such a thing. However, his new law gave Jews permission to defend themselves against those who tried to carry out Haman's wicked decree. And God was with the Jews and sent angels to protect them wherever they lived in the Persian Empire.

So ends the story of Esther. Everywhere that the tale is told, everyone remembers her faith in God and her courage to stand up for her people.

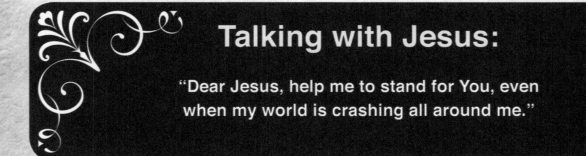

Talking with Jesus:

"Dear Jesus, help me to stand for You, even when my world is crashing all around me."

These aren't just storybooks

Each story includes a page with thought questions to help children apply the message in their own lives. These books will change your child's life—for good!

Order a set for your family today!

Bible stories aren't just for kids.

Are Adam and Eve, Noah and the flood, and Daniel in the lions' den still relevant in today's fast-paced world? Discover the deeper meaning behind familiar Bible stories in the five-volume *Century Classics Collection.* You'll be amazed at the life lessons found in these long-ago events!

You'll watch as world history unfolds from beginning to end, revealing a God who has done more for us than we can ever imagine.

What is the one thing He wants from us in return? These insightful books hold the answer.